Men are from Mars

Women are from Hell

John K. Chapman

Men are from Mars Women are from Hell© 2010, John K. Chapman. All rights reserved.

No part of this book may be used or reproduced in any form or by any means, or stored in a database or retrieval system without the prior written permission of the publisher, except in the case of brief quotations embodied in critical articles or reviews. Making copies of any part of this book for any purpose other than your own personal use is a violation of United States copyright laws. Entering any of the contents into a computer for mailing list or database purposes is strictly prohibited unless written authorization is obtained from the owner.

Introduction

Originally this was to be a collection of woman bashing jokes. I put a pen and paper on my nightstand and started with the following observation:

Women's most common complaint about their mates is leaving the toilet seat up. She goes to use the toilet and falls into the water. That can certainly be upsetting. The problem is that she gets upset with the man. In my opinion anyone who sets their naked ass down on something without looking first, is stupid.

That was what I intended to build the book from. The theme was to be a put down of the 'fairer sex'. Then I began to surprise myself. Women don't laugh at jokes they think are gross; like 'the pig with the wooden leg', the way men will. They will laugh at jokes that make them feel superior; like 'the suddenly over confident, sexist midget'.

It was easy to find jokes that made women look stupid. There's certainly abundance of dumb blonde jokes. For some reason all the dumb blondes are female. Men seem to enjoy jokes more than women.

On the other hand men are not immune from stupidity no matter how much we like to pretend that we are the smarter sex. This turned into a learning experience for me.

It comes down to the essences of comedy. Think about it. We laugh when we are made to feel superior. Remember the little moron jokes, the Polish jokes, and of course the dumb blonde jokes?

We laugh when we are told about someone doing something stupid; doing something we know better than to do. We laugh at ignorance. We laugh at people who don't know what we know. It makes us feel smart. It makes us feel superior. That makes us laugh.

Damn. Comedy is kind of sad.

So, now I determined that not only do we laugh at what makes us feel superior, but also that those things can be dramatically different from men to women. Obviously men and women are different. Different doesn't mean superior or inferior

Girls grow up playing with dolls and learning to appreciate frilly clothes. They learned to turn up their noses at "gross" things. They're conditioned to behave like girls as men are the converse. This is the way it's always been.

With all of this said, we understand why most jokes are predictable, but there are a few surprises here. There is also some interesting social commentary. Much is taken from famous people you think you know. Then some is from yours truly.

While there are some sexist anecdotes here for sure, they are done with a smile and a wink, along with some fun poked at men as well.

While the title does say "Women are from Hell", it doesn't say or mean to imply that men are from Heaven. Mars can be a goofy place as well.

Special Thanks

It was my good fortune to be introduced to Tom Shubnell. To date Tom has thirty nine joke books published plus several books in his field of health care information technology. He just started an exciting project with electronic joke books.

When Tom learned that I had an interest in writing a book like this he volunteered his services to help make this happen. In addition to getting this published he led me by the hand in setting up my computer and tutoring me on an almost daily basis.

Tom even came up with the cover which I think is really good; a long, rough, and fiery road between Mars and hell.

Thank you, Tom.

Tom has a blog at shubsthoughts.com. You'll find a lot of interesting material, information on his books and how to get a free subscription to his Friday Thoughts.

Table of Contents

Pig with a Wooden Leg 2

Annie's Joke 4

A Great Weekend 6

More on Pigs 8

Stuff 9

Cutbacks 11

Before and After Marriage 12

Professor 14

Merry Christmas 15

The Pirate's Duck 16

Differences 17

Quotes 20

Dorothy Parker 23

More Quotes 25

Mae West 32

And More Quotes 36

Thoughts from Dolly Parton 50

Other Thoughts 51

The Plane Trip 57

Geography of Women 58

More Thoughts 59

A Woman's Poem 61

Best Line in a Country Song 62

Best Headline 63

Got Away Cold 64

Viagra 65

Viagra to Save the Marriage 66

Cute Mistress 67

The Beginning 68

Quickies 69

Words with Two Meanings 77

The Class Reunion 78

He said, She said 79

And Then it Started 81

Male 82

Women's Seminar Topics 86

Poetry 87

Marine Corps Drinking Song 90

More Quickies 91

Dear Mom 95

Graffiti 96

Freudian Slip 97

Profound Thoughts 98

Deserted Island 102

Women's Vocabulary Lesson for Men 103

Riddles 104

Some Differences 105

Gotta Love Southwest Airlines 113

Christmas Ham 114

Cheating Wife 115

The Young Air Policeman 116

Golf Story 117

Divorce 118

Poor Farmer 119

The Road Trip 120

Texas Gal 121

Costume Party 123

Frank Felman 125

George W.	127
Women with Big Breasts	128
Women with Small Breasts	129
Short Ones	130
Maria Gets a Raise	133
Getting a Ticket	134
Sorority Girls	137
Public Works	140
Women's Rules	141
Men's Rules	143
Thoughts from Groucho	146
A Woman's Perfect Breakfast	147
The Beltline Office	148
Still Got a Sense of Humor	151
Man of the House	157
Great Women's Tee-Shirts	158
One Liners	163
Hanoi Jane	170
Women are Vindictive	174
Manly Test	175

How to Get Along 179

Advice from Men to Women 180

True Story Received from an English Professor.............. 182

Perfect Day for a Man 185

Perfect Day for a Woman 187

Pig with a Wooden Leg

This first joke is a classic in illustrating the differences in the senses of humor between the sexes. Most men find it hilarious while almost every female that hears it, thinks it's disgusting.

Going down a country road, a traveler spots what appears to be a pig with a wooden leg. He goes back and sure enough there it is in the barnyard.

He pulls into the lane and finds the farmer working on a piece of equipment. He introduces himself and asks, "Why in the world does that pig have a wooden leg?"

The farmer explains, "Son, that there ain't any ordinary pig. Last month we was about to lose this farm. That pig, right there, took hold of my wife's apron string and pulled her down into that holler back there. He took her to a big growth of truffles, which turned out to be an expensive variety. We harvested those truffles and sold them for enough money to pay all our bills and put some money in the bank. That pig kept us from the poor house.

"That's a wonderful story but why does he have a wooden leg?" the traveler asks again.

"And that's not all," continues the farmer, "The other night our house caught fire. That pig some how broke out of the pen, climbed the porch steps, pushed the door open, came upstairs where the wife and me was sleeping and kept bumping the bed until we woke up. That pig saved us and the house from burning up. Why son, besides that . . ."

The traveler interrupts, "Sir, I'm sure that that's another wonderful story, but what I want to know is; why does he have a wooden leg?"

"Son, a pig that special, you don't eat him all at once."

Valadation

My confidence really got a boost when, shortly after this book was written, I saw Jay Leno discussing comedy with a young comic who was working on material on women's senses of humor. Jay says, "Of course you've got to include the classic, 'pig with a wooden leg' joke."

In addition to being the long time host of the "Tonight Show" Jay does an amazing number of play dates as a stand up comic because he loves it. I view him as the utmost authority on comedy.

Annie's Joke

I have to give Annie Gill credit for this one. Annie married my best friend in the Marine Corps, Lynn Gill. Annie only had this one joke, but her delivery was flawless. At parties there was always a request of, "Annie, tell your joke."

This is included here, because while it gets a laugh from everyone, I've noticed that women find it especially funny. In fact it is so well received by the fairer sex it offers some insight into what makes women laugh.

This midget goes to a shrink. (*No, that's not the joke.*) "Doctor, I'm seriously considering suicide."

The doctor replies, "Oh no, you don't want to do that. Tell me about yourself. What do you do for a living?"

"I work on Wall Street. I'm at the top of my field. I'm written up in all the financial publications on a regular basis. I manage several billion dollars in assets and typically make ten to twelve million a year."

The doctor says, "That's great. What's the problem?"

"I'm forty years and I can't develop a serious relationship with a woman. I'm three feet tall for heavens sake. Women won't take me seriously. They pat me on the head, talk baby talk to me. I'm really thinking about just ending it all."

"No, no, don't do that. It doesn't matter how tall or short, big or small you are. If you stand up straight, hold your head up, your shoulders back, chest out, and walk and talk with confidence, people will react to you in kind." The doctor goes on to give him a rousing motivational talk.

After the midget leaves, he stops for a drink with his new found confidence. He kicks a bar stool where a rather large fellow is sitting and barks "This is where I like to sit." The big guy scrambles to another spot.

The midget climbs up to sit on the bar stool, slams his fist on the bar and loudly calls to the bartender, "I want a martini. It'd better be extra dry. It'd better be top shelf and it better be now." The bartender immediately starts working as fast as he can to fill the order just right.

Just then a beautiful lady takes the seat next to the midget. (*I have fun telling this joke when there's a girl in the audience by commenting, 'Almost as beautiful as you'.*)

The midget, now the most confident he's been in his life, looks over and up to the lady and boldly asks, "Hey good lookin', what would you say to a little fuck?"

The lady smugly looks down at the midget and says, "Hello little fuck."

A Great Weekend

I've had a lot of fun telling this joke over the years. It works best told to a group which includes some females.

As a little background, this was told to me by Omar Butari, a fellow trainee at the school Ross Perot set up for the stock brokerage firm he took over in the early seventies. Omar's family owned a Maserati dealership in Miami.

Omar was working a car show one Saturday when he sees a couple looking at one of his cars. It's about a two hundred thousand dollar car, in today's dollars.

The gentleman is older, silver haired, dressed casually but very well groomed. He looks wealthy, Palm Beach style. The young lady on his arm is drop dead gorgeous, centerfold material. As Omar approaches them, the man is asking his date if she likes this car. She says she loves it.

Omar introduces himself and begins answering questions about the car. Every other question the gentleman asks the girl if she really likes the car, the car's interior, the color, etc. She likes the car, big time.

He asks Omar if it'll pull a Cigarette. That's an off shore racing boat that sells for two hundred grand and up. Omar tells him, yes, it'll pull it real fast. You just have to make sure the trailer hitch is properly mounted.

The man asks if he can put on the hitch. Omar says they can have it ready mid-day Monday.

They agree on a price and the man gives Omar a check for fifty thousand dollars with the balance to be paid when they pick up the car Monday. As they leave the girl is walking on air.

The next day at the yacht club Omar runs into the guy who has the local Cigarette dealership and relates the sale he made at the car show. The boat dealer exclaims that the same guy bought the girl a two hundred and some thousand dollar boat the same day.

They figure he spent maybe a half million dollars on this girl that Saturday and the boat dealer says the fellow just met her Friday night. (*At this point most of the ladies in the audience are shaking their heads at why they can't meet a guy like that.*)

When Omar goes into the dealership Monday morning our gentleman is on the phone. He says he hopes they haven't started installing the hitch, because he can't take the car. He says he hopes Omar hasn't made a bank deposit since his check is no good. He goes on to apologize for the trouble he's caused.

"But mainly," he says, "I want to thank you for helping an old man have one of the greatest weekends of his life."

Now comes the fun part; watching the expressions on the faces of the jealous girls in your audience. I've told this joke for many years. Most of that time, I felt a little sorry for the girl being made a fool. Then it dawned on me that this old fellow was such a pro that the girl probably never realized that she'd been played.

Somewhere there is an aging beauty remembering the magic weekend when she almost hit the jackpot, but something she said or did turned him away.

More on Pigs

Here's another one that makes men laugh and women snort with disgust.

A city boy hitch hiking through the South, catches a ride on a farm truck hauling some hogs to market. As he and the farmer are talking, the farmer is astounded at the boy's lack of country life experiences.

"I bet you've never smelled fresh cut hay on a dewy morning. I bet you've never seen a newborn calf. Hell, I bet you've never even done it with a pig.

The boy admits that's all true.

"Son, doing it with a pig is part of being a man. Shoot, I got a load of pigs right here. We'll just pull off the road here and bring you into manhood."

They climb into the back of the truck, where the farmer tells the boy to pick out one and follow his lead. The farmer drops his overalls, grabs a pig by the hind legs and gets at it. He looks over to the boy. The kid has his jeans down, holding a pig, but he's just standing there.

"What's the matter boy?"

"I don't know. I can't get it up."

"Lord God, no wonder boy! You got the ugliest one in the bunch!"

Stuff

Advertisement in the New York Post

For Sale by owner: Complete set of Encyclopedia Britannica. 45 volumes. Excellent condition. $1,000 or best offer.

No longer needed. Got married last weekend.

Wife knows everything.

Why we split up

She told me we couldn't afford beer anymore and I'd have to quit. Then I caught her spending $65 on make-up. So I asked, how come I had to give up stuff and not her.

She said she needed the make-up to look pretty for me.

I told her that was what the beer was for. I don't think she's coming back.

Happy Anniversary

"You think so much of golf that you don't even remember when we were married."

"Of course I do, my dear, it was the day I sank that forty-foot putt."

Good basis for marriage?

Counseling

A husband and wife were at a party chatting with some friends when the subject of marriage counseling came up.

"Oh, we'll never need that. My husband and I have a great relationship," the wife explained. "He was a communications major in college and I majored in theatre arts. He communicates really well and I just act like I'm listening."

Why so grouchy? Got a flat tire on your menstrual cycle?

It's all about the bitches.

--American Kennel Club slogan, (*possibility*)

A rodeo cowboy was asked why he chose to make his living in such a dangerous activity as wild bull riding.

His classic response was, "It's pretty simple. I'm too lazy to work, too nervous to steal and too jealous to pimp."

Cutbacks

The manager is informed that he must reduce his staff by one. After agonizing over this difficult chore, he narrows the candidates to two, very equal employees; a male and a female. Let's call them Jack and Jill.

He thought he would fire the employee who came late to work the next morning. Both Jack and Jill came to work very early.

Then the manager thought he would catch the first one who took a coffee break. Unfortunately, neither Jack nor Jill took a coffee break that day.

Then the manager decided to see who took the longest lunch break. It was a bad day for him as neither Jack nor Jill took a lunch break that day. They both ate at their desk.

Then the manager thought he would wait and see who would leave work the earliest. Again he was confounded because both employees stayed until after closing.

Jill finally went to the coat rack so the manager thought he would simply be honest and ask her advice.

He went up to her and said, "Jill, I have a terrible problem. I don't know whether to lay you or Jack off."

Jill said, "I hope you'll just jack off. I've got a headache"

Before and After Marriage

Before - You take my breath away.
After - I feel like I'm suffocating.

Before - Twice a night.
After - Twice a month.

Before - She loves the way I take control of a Situation.
After - She called me a controlling, manipulative, egomaniac.

Before - Ricky & Lucy.
After - Fred & Ethel.

Before - Saturday Night Live.
After - Monday Night Football.

Before - He makes me feel like a million dollars.
After - If I had a dime for every stupid thing he's done. . .

Before - Don't Stop.
After - Don't Start.

Before - The Sound of Music.
After - The Sound of Silence.

Before - Is that all you are eating?
After - Maybe you should just have a salad, honey.

Before - Wheel of Fortune.
After - Jeopardy.

Before - It's like living a dream.
After - It's a nightmare.

Before - $60/dozen.
After - $1.50/stem.

Before - Turbocharged.
After - Needs a jump-start.

Before - Victoria's Secret.
After - Fruit of the Loom.

Before - Feathers & handcuffs.
After - Ball and chain.

Before - Idol.
After - Idle.

Before - He's lost without me.
After - Why can't he ask for directions?

Before - When together, time stands still.
After - This relationship is going nowhere.

Before - Croissant and cappuccino.
After - Bagels and instant coffee.

Before - Oysters.
After - Fish sticks.

Before - I can hardly believe we found each other.
After - How the hell did I end up with someone like you?

Before - Romeo and Juliet.
After - Bill and Hillary.

Professor

My Alma Mater, Western Kentucky University was formerly Western Kentucky State College and before that it was Western Kentucky State Teacher's College.

Of course, back then most of the teaching students were women and also at that time it was considered very bad form to use bad language or tell anything close to an off-color joke in front of a female.

There was one crusty old professor who loved to shock the young ladies in his class by telling racy jokes.

One girl got all of her fellow coeds together teach him a lesson. They agreed that the next time he started to tell one of these jokes they would all get up and leave the room.

There were a few guys in the class and they loved the old fellow. Of course, they tipped him off.

So beginning the next class he announces, "Girls, have I got a good one for you today."

The leader of the group looked around and all the girls scooted to the edge of their seats getting ready for the dirty joke to start so they could get up and walk out of the class.

The professor starts with, "Did you hear about the boatload of whores leaving for China?"

That's it. They all get up and head for the door.

The professor calls after them, "There's no rush ladies. The boat doesn't leave for two months."

Merry Christmas

It was during Christmas season when the beautiful young housewife, in a sexy negligee, opened the door to the mailman. She gives him a big kiss then takes him upstairs and makes wild passionate love to him.

After he gets dressed, he comes downstairs to find that she has prepared him a full blown breakfast; eggs Benedict, French toast, hash browns, fresh squeezed juice, gourmet coffee, everything.

When he finishes, she walks him to the door, kisses him good bye and wishes him a Merry Christmas as she puts a dollar bill in his pocket.

The postman is flabbergasted. "In all my years I've never had a Christmas gift like this. Thank you, but why?"

"As we were going over our Christmas list, I asked my husband, what should we do for the mailman?"

He said, "Fuck him. Give him a dollar."

"Breakfast was my idea."

The Pirate's Duck

A drunk someway or another in his travels of the evening ends up with a duck. He is very taken with this duck because it will sit on his shoulder like a pirate's parrot. He thinks this is the coolest thing he's ever seen!

So he gets home, stumbles into the bedroom, turns on the light where his wife is sleeping, wakes her up and loudly asks, "Hey, what do you think about my pig?"

She snorts, "You drunken bastard, that's not a pig, that's a duck."

He slurs, "I know. I was asking the duck."

Differences

My wife wanted a boob job. She got upset, because I could only afford for her to get one done at a time.

She really got upset when I suggested she rub toilet paper between them. She asked if that would make them larger. I answered, "Well it worked on your ass."

Here's something to think about: If Mama Cass had shared that sandwich with Karen Carpenter, they might both be alive today.

What does Courtney Love have in common with a hockey team?

They both take a shower after three periods.

A drunk watches intently as the checker rings up the items for the lady ahead of him at the market; jar of instant coffee, half dozen eggs, loaf of bread, and a box of tampons.

He slurs, "You're single aren't you?"

The lady replies, "Yes. How could you tell?"

The drunk says, "You're ugly."

The main reason women get married; somebody asked them.

Do you not know I am a woman? When I think I must speak.
- *As You Like It, Act 3, Scene 2*

Women always worry about things men forget

Men always worry about things women remember

There are three kinds of men who don't understand women:

Young, old, and middle aged.

A man will pay two dollars for a one dollar item he needs,

A woman will pay one dollar for a two dollar item she doesn't need.

Why are married women heavier than single women?

Single women come home, see what's in the fridge and go to bed.

Married women come home, see what's in bed and go to the fridge.

My journey through life

When I was 13, I hoped that one day I'd have a girlfriend with big tits.

At 16 I got a girlfriend with big tits but there was no passion. I decided I needed a passionate girl with a zest for life.

In college I dated a passionate girl but she was too emotional. Everything was a crisis. She was a drama queen. She cried all the time and even threatened suicide. I decided I needed a girlfriend with stability

A 25 I found a very stable girl but she was boring and never got excited about anything. Life was dull so I decided that I needed a girl with some excitement.

At 30 I found an exciting girl but I couldn't keep up with her. She did impetuous things and made me miserable more often than she made me happy. I decided to find a girl with ambition.

At 40 I found a smart ambitious girl with her feet planted firmly on the ground. She was so ambitious that she sued me for divorce and took everything I had.

I am older and wiser now so I'm looking for a girl with big tits.

Quotes

This first quote had a lot to do with this book being written. It still amazes me that it came from a proper English Lord and famous poet a few hundred years ago. Even women agree that it's profound.

I don't understand women. I don't want to understand women, because women understand women, and they don't like them.

- Lord Byron

Men think about women. Women think about what men think about them.

-Peter Ustinov

Women are like elephants. I like to look at them, but I wouldn't want to own one.

-W.C. Fields

Women are like ovens. We need 5-15 minutes to warm up.

-Sandra Bullock

Absence – the common cure of love.

-Lord Byron

I don't know why women want any of the things that men have, when the one thing that women have is men.

-Coco Channel

I've always found women difficult. I don't understand them. To begin with, few women will tell the truth.

-Barbara Cartwell

I've always liked men better than women.

-Bette Davis

Strong women marry weak men.

-Bette Davis

If women didn't exist, all the money in the world would have no meaning.

-Aristotle Onassis

Women are nothing but machines for producing children.

-Napoleon Bonaparte

I see that you've been married to the same woman for sixty years. That must be very *inexpensive*.

-Johnny Carson

Sometimes it's hard to be a woman.

-Tammy Wynette

Dorothy Parker

Dorothy Parker was very popular in the 1920's as a writer for the New Yorker, Vanity Fair, and many literary journals. She had over 300 poems published, countless articles, and even wrote Hollywood screen plays. Always outspoken with a quick mind, she was asked to leave a Catholic elementary school when she referred to the Immaculate Conception as 'spontaneous combustion'. Her formal education ended at age 13. Many of her most infamous quips were made at cocktail parties or while drinking with fellow writers. Here are some of my favorites.

I only require three things of a man: He must be handsome, ruthless, and stupid.

If all the girls who attended the Yale prom were laid end to end, I wouldn't be a bit surprised.

It serves me right for keeping all my eggs in one bastard

I like to have a martini;

Two at the very most.

After three I'm under the table;

After four, I'm under the host

I'd rather have a bottle in front of me than a frontal lobotomy.

You can lead a horticulture, but you can't make her think.

Ducking for apples. Change one letter and it's the story of my life.

This would be a good thing to put on my tombstone: Everywhere she went, including here, was against her better judgment.

Scratch a lover and find a foe.

Tell him I'm fucking busy, or vice versa.

More Quotes

I hate housework. You make the beds and do the dishes. Then six months later you have to start all over again.

-Joan Rivers

The secret to staying young is live honestly, eat slowly, and lie about your age.

-Lucille Ball

Women's lib doesn't interest me one bit. I've been so liberated, it hurts.

-Lucille Ball

A man who correctly guesses a woman's age may be smart, but not very bright.

-Lucille Ball

I don't do T & A very well because I don't have much of either.

-Lucille Ball

I have flabby thighs, but fortunately, my stomach covers them.

-Joan Rivers

I don't think I'm good in bed. My husband never said anything, but after we'd make love, he would take a piece of chalk and outline my body.

-Joan Rivers

Seize the moment. Remember all the women on the Titanic who waved off the dessert cart.

-Erma Bombeck

Experts say you should never hit your children in anger. When is a good time, when you're feeling festive?

-Roseanne Barr

I consider myself to be a pretty good judge of people. That's why I don't like any of them.

-Roseanne Barr

I figure if my kids are alive at the end of the day, I've done my job.

-Roseanne Barr

The quickest way to a man's heart is through his chest.

-Roseanne Barr

Women complain about PMS, but I think of it as the only time of the month that I can be myself.

-Roseanne Barr

My hope is that gays will be running the world because then there will be no war - Just a greater emphasis on military apparel.

-Roseanne Barr

Before marriage a girl has make love to a man to hold him. After marriage, she has to hold him to make love to him.

-Marilyn Monroe

Hollywood is a place where they pay you $1,000 for a kiss and 50 cents for your soul.

-Marilyn Monroe

Husbands are chiefly good as lovers when they are betraying their wives.

-Marilyn Monroe

I don't mind living in a man's world as long as I can be a woman in it.

-Marilyn Monroe

I've been on a calendar, but I've never been on time.

-Marilyn Monroe

It's better to be unhappy alone than unhappy with someone – so far.

-Marilyn Monroe

It's not true that I had nothing on – I had the radio on.

-Marilyn Monroe

What do I wear in bed? Why, Chanel #5 of course.

-Marilyn Monroe

If you always do what interest you, at least one person is pleased.

-Katharine Hepburn

If you want to sacrifice the admiration of many men for the criticism of one, go ahead, get married.

-Katharine Hepburn

Life is hard , , , after all, it kills you.

-Katharine Hepburn

Plain women know more about men than beautiful women do.

-Katharine Hepburn

Darling, these legs aren't so beautiful. I just know what to do with them.

-Marlene Dietrich

I am at heart a gentleman.

-Marlene Dietrich

Most women set out to try to change a man, and when they change him, they do not like him.

-Marlene Dietrich

Once a woman has forgiven her man, she must not re-heat his sins for breakfast.

-Marlene Dietrich

A husband is what is left of a lover after the nerve has been extracted.

-Helen Rowland

God will get you for that, Walter.

-Bea Arthur, *as Maude*

You see a lot of smart men with dumb women but you never see a smart woman with a dumb man.

-Erica Jong

Being a woman is a matter of life after death; now that he's dead, I have a life.

-Madeline Kahn

I never married because there was no need. I have three pets at home which serve the same purposes as a husband. I have a dog which growls every morning, a parrot which swears every afternoon and a cat that come home late at night.

-Marie Corelli

When I was married to Cary Grant. . .

-A lead in line that Dyan Cannon used in order to boost her image every time she was interviewed until it was rumored that he was gay.

Sure, marriage can be fun some of the time. Trouble is you're married all of the time.

-Maxine

Mae West

Mae West got her first break in 1918 with Ed Wynn on Broadway. Later she wrote, produced, directed, and starred in a play she titled Sex. Police raided the theater and arrested her on charges of 'corrupting the morals of youth'. The publicity caused her career to ignite. She is still known for what were considered very racy comments. Here are some of my favorites.

A hard man is good to find.

Too much of a good thing can be wonderful.

A man may be short and dumpy and getting bald, but if he has fire, women will like him.

A man in the house is worth two in the street.

All discarded lovers should be given a second chance, but with someone else.

An ounce of performance is worth pounds of promises.

Any time you have nothing to do, and lots of time to do it, come on up.

Anything worth doing is worth doing slowly.

When women go wrong, men go right after them.

Between two evils I always pick the one I've never tried before.

Don't keep a man guessing too long. He's sure to find the answer somewhere else.

Don't marry a man to reform him. That's what reform schools are for.

Every man I meet wants to protect me. I can't figure out what from.

Give a man a free hand and he will run it all over you.

He is the kind of man a woman would have to marry to get rid of.

I believe that it's better to be looked over than be overlooked.

I generally avoid temptation unless I can't resist it.

I like a man who is good but not too good – because the good die young and I hate a dead one.

I never worry about diets. The only carrots that interest me are the number you get in a diamond.

I only have yes men around me. Who needs no men?

I only like two kinds of men – domestic and imported.

I know two languages – body and English.

I used to be Snow White, but I drifted.

I'd like to see Paris before I die. Philadelphia will do.

I don't know much about politics but I can recognize a good party man when I see one.

I'll try anything once, twice, if I like it, three times to make sure.

I'm a lady of very few words but lots of action.

I'm no model lady. A model is just an imitation of the real thing.

I've been in more laps than a napkin.

I've been things and seen places.

It ain't no sin if you crack a few laws every now and again just so long as you don't break any.

It takes two to get one in trouble.

It's not the men in my life it's the life in my men.

Opportunity knocks for every man, but you have to give a woman a ring.

Save a boyfriend for a rainy day and another in case it doesn't rain.

Sex is emotion in motion.

She's the kind of girl who climbed the ladder of success wrong by wrong.

Ten men are waiting for me at the door? Send one of them home, I'm tired.

The score never interested me – only the game.

Those who are easily shocked should be shocked more often.

To err is human but it feels divine.

Too much of a good thing can be wonderful.

His mother should have thrown him away and kept the stork.

Virtue has its own reward but no sale at the box office.

You only live once, but if you do it right, once is enough.

And More Quotes

Adopted kids are such a pain – you have to teach them how to look like you

-Gilda Radner

I base most of my fashion taste on what doesn't itch.

-Gilda Radner

I'm so full I can't hear.

-Gilda Radner

I love playing bitches. There's a lot in every woman – a lot in every man.

- Joan Crawford

I need sex for a clear complexion but I'd rather do it for love.

-Joan Crawford

I never go outside unless I look like Joan Crawford the movie star. If you want to see the girl next door, go next door.

-Joan Crawford

Woman's lib? Poor little things, they always look so unhappy. Have you noticed how bitter their faces are?

-Joan Crawford

The day I worry about cleaning my house is the day Sears comes out with a riding vacuum cleaner.

-Roseanne

They say I'm a bitch, like that's a bad thing.

-Roseanne

A man may be a fool and not know it but not if he is married.

-H.L. Mencken

A wedding is just like a funeral except you get to smell your own flowers.

-Grace Hansen

All marriages are happy – it's the living together afterward that causes all the trouble.

-Raymond Hull

Bachelors know more about women than married men. If they didn't they'd be married too.

-H.L. Mencken

I'm a marvelous housekeeper. Every time I leave a man, I keep the house.

-Zsa Zsa Gabor

Men are taught to apologize for their weaknesses, women for their strengths.

-Gloria Steinem

I have yet to hear a man ask for advice on how to combine marriage and a career.

-Gloria Steinem

A woman without a man is like a fish without a bicycle.

-Gloria Steinem

I'm tough, ambitious, and I know exactly what I want. If that makes me a bitch, okay.

-Madonna

If they can send a man to mars why can't they send them all?

-Lady Nancy Astor

Women are the only oppressed group in our society that lives in close association with their oppressors.

-Evelyn Cunningham

Do you know what it means to come home at night to a woman who will give you a little love, a little affection, a little tenderness? It means you're in the wrong house, that's what it means.

-Henny Youngman

My best birth control now is to leave the lights on.

-Joan Rivers

Getting divorced just because you don't love a man is almost as silly as getting married just because you do.

-Zsa Zsa Gabor

I have great hopes that we shall love each other all our lives as much as if we had never married at all.

-Lord Byron

I have learned that only two things are necessary to keep ones wife happy: First let her think she is having her own way. Second, let her have it.

-Lyndon B. Johnson

I've been married to one Marxist and one Fascist and neither one would take the garbage out.

-Lee Grant

If you want to read about love and marriage you have to buy two separate books.

-Allan King

I've been on so many blind dates I should get a free dog.

-Wendy Liebman

If you made a list of why any couple got married and another list for their divorce you'd have a lot of overlapping.

-Mignon McLaughlin

My boyfriend wanted to get married but I didn't want him to.

-Rita Rudner

Whenever I meet a man I ask myself, is that the man I want my children to spend their weekends with?

-Rita Rudner

I make love to twenty thousand people from the stage then go home alone.

-Janis Joplin

Question: If you could live forever, would you, and why?

Answer: "I would not live forever, because we should not live forever, because if we were supposed to live forever, then we would live forever, but we cannot live forever, which is why I would not live forever."

-Miss Alabama in the 1994 Miss USA contest.

Whenever I watch TV and see those poor starving kids all over the world, I can't help but cry. I mean I'd love to be skinny like that, but not with all those flies and death and stuff."

-Mariah Carey

Smoking kills. If you're killed, you've lost a very important part of your life,"

-Brooke Shields, during an interview to become spokesperson for federal anti-smoking campaign.

Jane, you ignorant slut!

-Chevy Chase, *Saturday Night Live*

Of the thousands of women that I've had, you're definitely in the top twenty percent.

- Charlie Sheen to Denise Richards, his soon to be ex-wife.

As if that didn't piss off enough women, he followed up with:

I never paid women for sex. I paid them to leave.

I actually witnessed this. Sitting with his fiancé, this nitwit lovingly says to her, "I've always been known for only going with beautiful women, but for some reason I've fallen in love with you." He wonders why she left him.

If it's inevitable, just relax and enjoy it.

-Clayton Williams, unsuccessful candidate for governor of Texas, comparing rape to the weather.

It isn't pollution that's harming the environment. It's the impurities in our air and water that are doing it."

-Al Gore, (*almost President*)

When the stock market crashed, Franklin Roosevelt got on the television and didn't talk about the princes of greed. He said, "Look, here's what happened."

-Joe Biden, (a heartbeat from being president)

They misunderestimated me.

-George W. Bush, President

Over the last 15 months, we've traveled to every corner of the United States. I've now been in 57 states? I think there's one left to go.

-Barack Obama, on the presidential campaign trail –

Oops, got off track for a minute there.

"It'll be my luck that doctors will conclude that there is no such thing as PMS, and I really am a bitch."

-*Most any woman*

I like my women just a little on the trashy side.

-Jerry Jeff Walker, *song title*

Beauty is in the eye of the beer holder.

-Kinky Friedman

I support gay marriage. I believe they have the right to be as miserable as the rest of us.

-Kinky Friedman

Get your biscuits in the oven and your buns in the bed.

-Kinky Friedman, *song title*

My wife knows what I like. I know what she won't do.

-Ron White

-Ron followed up with:

The first item on the list is, we don't talk about the list.

My wife and I practice doggy style sex. I beg and she rolls over.

-Steve Rice

My girlfriend always laughs during sex. . . no matter what she's reading.

-Steve Jobs, *founder of Apple Computer*

My wife is immature. I'll be in the bath tub and she'll come in and sink all my toy boats.

-Woody Allen

My sex life is terrible. The last time I was inside a woman was when I visited the Statue of Liberty.

-Woody Allen

My mother was like a sister to me only we didn't have sex as often.

-Emo Phillips

My classmates would copulate with anything that moved but I never saw any reason to limit myself.

-Emo Phillips

There's one thing I would break up over; if she caught me with another woman. I wouldn't stand for that.

-Steve Martin

Don't have sex, man. It leads to kissing and the next thing you'll have to start talking to them.

-Steve Martin

Women need a reason to have sex. Men just need a place.

-Billy Crystal

Ah yes, divorce, from the Latin word; meaning to rip out a man's genitals through his wallet.

-Robin Williams

Bigamy is having one wife too many. Monogamy is the same.

-Orson Welles

All the women on *The Apprentice* flirted with me - consciously or subconsciously. That's to be expected.

-Donald Trump

Every man wants to sink into a woman's arms without falling into her hands.

-Jerry Lee Lewis

Stifle yourself, Dingbat.

-Archie Bunker

I was married by a judge. I should have asked for a jury.

-George Burns

Ann Landers said that you are addicted to sex if you have sex more than three times a day and you should seek professional help. For me to have sex three times a day, I'd have to have professional help.

-Jay Leno

Getting married for sex is like buying a 737 for the free peanuts.

-Jeff Foxworthy

My wife is a sex object. Every time I ask for sex, she objects.

-Les Dawson

Being with a woman all night never hurt no baseball player. It's the staying out all night looking for 'em that does him in.

-Casey Stengel

You gotta learn that if you don't get it by midnight, chances are you ain't gonna get it, and if you do get it, it ain't worth it.

-Casey Stengel

Madame, I may be drunk, but in the morning I'll be sober and you'll still be ugly.

-Winston Churchill

Being powerful is like being a lady. If you have to tell people you are, you aren't.

-Margaret Thatcher

Thoughts from Dolly Parton

"I'm not offended by dumb blonde jokes because I know that I'm not dumb. I also know that I'm not blonde."

"You'd be surprised how much it costs to look this cheap."

"I describe my look as a combination of Mother Goose, Cinderella and the local hooker."

"I have little feet because nothing grows in the shade."

"After Momma gave birth to twelve of us kids, we put her up on a pedestal. It was mostly to keep Daddy away from her."

(on the topic of her breast size) "People always ask me if they're mine. Yes they are. . . all bought and paid for."

"There're plenty of charities for the homeless. Isn't it time somebody did something for the homely?"

"It's a good thing I was born a girl; otherwise I'd be a drag queen."

"I modeled my looks on the town tramp."

Other Thoughts

The wife was marveling about a football player who stood five feet nine inches and weighed two hundred and eighty pounds.

"That'll be me if I continue my eating habits", she commented.

"No, not you," he assured her, "You'll never be five foot nine."

In olden times, sacrifices were made at the altar, a practice which is continued today.

A woman arrived at a party and while scanning the guests spotted an attractive man standing alone. She approached him, smiled and said, "Hello, my name is Carmen."

"That's a beautiful name," he replied. "Is it a family name?"

"No," she replied. "Actually I gave it to myself. It represents the things that I enjoy the most - cars and men. Therefore, I chose Carmen."

"What's your name?"

He answered, "B.J. Titsengolf."

He was sweating like a blind lesbian in a fish market.

My wife said that I don't like her family. I told her that wasn't true. In fact, I like her mother in law better than mine.

The main thing money does is keep you from worrying about not having any money.

Don't confuse fame with success. Madonna is one, Helen Keller is the other.

A Jewish woman says to her mother, "I'm divorcing Sheldon. All he wants is anal sex. My ass hole is now the size of a quarter. It used to be about the size of a dime."

Her mother says, "You're married to a multi-millionaire businessman, you live in an 8 bedroom mansion, you drive a Ferrari, you get $1,000 a week allowance, you take 6 vacations a year and you want to throw all that away over 15 cents?"

She was plagued by a heavy breather on the phone for several weeks. One day he got the nerve to speak, "I'm sitting here naked. Guess what I have in my hand."

She replied, "If you can hold it in one hand I'm not interested."

He never called back.

Her house was so dirty you had to go outside to wipe your feet.

Women would be happy if men had big chocolate penises that ejaculated money.

The man had been slipping in and out of a coma for months yet his wife stayed by his bedside day and night. One day he came to and motioned for her to come nearer.

As she strained to hear, he whispered, "You've been with me through all the bad times. When I got shot you were there. When my business failed you were there. Through bankruptcy and failing health you were always there. You know what?"

Her heart swelled as she squeezed his hand and leaned in to better hear her husband of many years. "What dear?"

"You're bad luck."

Cell phones are the only thing I know of which men will brag to each other as to who has the smallest one.

Difference between a tire and a thousand used condoms:

One's a Goodyear, the other's a great year.

The caller says, "You probably don't even remember me but we met awhile back at the Singles Bar. We danced, drank, partied and had a wonderful time. You said you fell for me. I really fell for you. We spent the night together. You promised to call, but never did."

"Now I'm pregnant and there's no doubt it's yours. I just want you to know that when I put this phone down I'm going to kill myself. What do you have to say to that?"

"Oh baby! You're not only a good lay, you're a good sport."

Seriously, how can you trust anybody who bleeds five days every month and doesn't die?

A rich man spotted a beautiful young lady sitting alone at a singles bar. "Say, baby, how about you coming home with me and giving me some head?"

She barely looked up. "That'll be the day."

Undaunted, he tried again. "Well, then, what if we go to my place and screw like rabbits?"

This time she snickered. "That'll be the day!"

"Okay," he said, "How about we take my limo to my private jet, fly to Tahiti , and spend a week at my private beach?"

She looked up, smiled, and said, *"This will* be the day."

A guy approaches a hot cutie in the ski lodge. Trying to start a little conversation he comments, "My goodness, your ski pants are tight . How in the world do you get into them?"

"You could start by buying me a drink."

This chick with a great ass looked really good in her black leather mini skirt.

When she farted, it smelled like a new BMW.

Says his daughter must be a beauty queen.

She keeps saying she's Miss Understood.

Ideas for women's calling cards:

Modest tastes in food and clothing. Will pass the savings on to you.

Still time to bear children if we get busy.

I may be built like a Buick but I drive like a Mercedes

If I can make a dress out of a flour sack, I can make a man out of you.

Tip for our young Marines:

If you're ever hassled by a war protester, wink at his girlfriend. She knows he's a pussy.

A young and pretty women asked me if I liked breasts or thighs. I said that I really liked shaved snatches.

I'm not welcome back at KFC.

If women are such great multi taskers why can't they handle a headache and sex at the same time?

Did you hear that Elaine got married?

Married! Hell, I didn't even know she was pregnant.

Honey, There'll be no sex tonight. I'm tender from my gynecologist's visit.

You didn't go to the dentist too did you?

The Plane Trip

A plane passed through a severe storm. The turbulence was awful and things went from bad to worse when lighting struck the right wing.

One woman lost it completely. She stood up in the front of the plane and yelled, "If I'm going to die I want to die feeling like a woman. Is there any man here who can make me feel like a woman?"

In the back of the plane a tall, lean and handsome Texan quietly stood up. The plane went silent. All eyes were on him as he slowly made his way toward the woman.

He began unbuttoning his shirt. His bared chest was broad, tan and muscular.

The woman gasped.

As he approached, he handed her the shirt and said, "Iron this and get me a beer."

Geography of Women

Between 18 and 22, a woman is like Africa, half discovered, half wild, fertile and naturally beautiful!

Between 23 and 30, a woman is like Europe, well developed and open to trade, especially for someone with cash.

Between 31 and 35, a woman is like Spain, very hot, relaxed and convinced of her own beauty.

Between 36 and 40, a woman is like Greece, gently aging but still a warm and desirable place to visit.

Between 41 and 50, a woman is like Great Britain with a glorious and all conquering past.

Between 51 and 60, a woman is like Israel; has been through war and doesn't make the same mistakes twice, takes care of business

Between 61 and 70, a woman is like Canada, self-preserving but open to meeting new people.

After 70, she becomes like Tibet, wildly beautiful, with a mysterious past and the wisdom of the ages...only those with an adventurous spirit and a thirst for spiritual knowledge visit there.

Geography of Man

Between 10 and 80, a man is like Illinois, ruled by nuts...

More Thoughts

Women are smarter when they're having sex. They've got a brain plugged into them.

The average woman would rather be beautiful than smart because she knows that the average man can see better than he can think.

If variety is the spice of life; marriage is the leftover can of Spam.

Playboy is coming out with an edition for the married man. It has the same centerfold every month.

Of course married men live longer than single men. They're more willing to die.

Menstruation and menopause. . . notice that all women's problems start with men.

After an ugly breakup she sends him pictures of herself in bed with her new boyfriend. He forwards them to her dad.

Why is a woman like cow manure?

The older she gets, the easier she is to pick up.

You can reuse a condom. Just wash the fuck out of it.

When I was born, I was given a choice between a big penis or a great memory.

I don't remember which I chose.

He said that he'd had bad luck with marriage.

He said that his first wife left him and that his second wife didn't.

A Woman's Poem

Before I lay me down to sleep,
I pray for a man who's not a creep,

One who's handsome, smart and strong.
One who loves to listen long,

One who thinks before he speaks,
One who'll call, not wait for weeks.

I pray he's rich and self-employed,
And when I spend, won't be annoyed.

Pull out my chair and hold my hand,
Massage my feet and help me stand.

Oh send a king to make me queen.
A man who loves to cook and clean.

I pray this man will love no other,
And relish visits with my mother.

A Man's Poem

I pray for a deaf-mute gymnast nymphomaniac with big boobs who owns a bar on a golf course, and loves to send me fishing and drinking. This doesn't rhyme and I don't give a crap.

Best Line in a Country Song

I have loved some ladies and I have loved Jim Beam,

They both tried to kill me in 1973

--Hank Williams, jr. Lyrics in Family Tradition (and it don't even rhyme)

Remember; anyone can get laid or even married in short order if they lower their standards enough.

Personally, I'd rather not have what I want than to have what I don't want.

Best Headline

Back in 1994, rumors were abounding that Lisa Marie Presley and Michael Jackson had gotten married. Finally a press release was issued that, yes, they had, indeed married. The Dallas Morning News ran a photo of the happy couple on the front page of its Entertainment section. The headline read:

If Elvis isn't dead; this ought to do it

Shortly after Jackson's death there was a large thunderstorm prompting a comment of, "You know that's not thunder. That's Elvis kicking the shit out of Michael for marrying his daughter."

Got Away Cold

Two women meet standing in line at the pearly gates and strike up a conversation.

Woman One asks, "You're a relatively young lady. How in the world did you die so young?"

Woman Two replies: "I froze to death."

Woman One: "Gosh, that sounds terrible!"

Woman Two: "Actually, it's not that bad. It doesn't take very long to get over being cold and then you just basically fall asleep. How about yourself, how did you die?"

Woman One: "I had a massive heart attack."

Woman Two: "My goodness, did something cause that?"

Woman One: "Oh, yeah, I had this feeling that my husband was cheating on me. I work downtown and he works at home. One day I slipped home to catch him. I had some trouble getting the garage door open and he must have heard me. Anyway, I walk in and he's sitting in the den, and he never sits in the den. He looks suspicious, so I'm just sure he has a woman in the house. I tear through the house and search every room and closet. I run upstairs and search through every room upstairs. I climb through the attic door and search every square inch of the attic. I come back down, go to the basement and search all of that. Then I run back up and do it all again, until finally, I guess I just ran myself to death."

Woman Two: "Wow! You know?. . .We might both be alive today if you had just looked in the deep freeze."

Viagra

A man goes to the doctor to get some Viagra. The doctor explains that this is a serious medication. Many things must be considered first. The doctor asks him to bring in his wife for further consultation.

The man brings in his wife and the doctor asks to meet with her alone. They go into an examination room, where he asks her to disrobe. He has her turn around then he has her get on the table and turn several different ways. He tells her to get dressed while he talks to the husband.

The doctor says to the husband, "There's nothing wrong with you. I couldn't get an erection either."

A girl bitching to a guy about the double standard whines, "It's so wrong. When a man screws a lot of women, he's a stud. When a girl does a lot of men she's a slut".

The guy replies, "It's like when a key opens a lot of locks it's called a master key. When a lock is opened by a lot of keys it's called a cheap lock."

Viagra to Save the Marriage

A man goes to his old college buddy who's now an M.D. to get some Viagra, to help get his marriage back on track. The drug had just come out and was in short supply.

The doctor says that he only has one pill on hand and asks how long his drive home is. When the man says thirty minutes, the doc says, "That's perfect. Take it now. It'll kick in within about forty five minutes."

Half an hour later the doc gets a frantic call from his college pal. "My wife's not home. She's gone to Houston to tend to her sick mother. Now that pill's going to be wasted."

The doc asks, "Isn't there someone you can use it with?"

"Yeah, there's the maid, but I don't need the Viagra for her."

A side effect of Viagra: The wife gets a headache.

Love is blind. Marriage is the eye opener.

Cute Mistress

A husband and wife are having dinner in a nice restaurant when a beautiful young lady stops by and says to the husband, "I must say, you look exceptionally handsome this evening."

I hope I can look forward to seeing you a little later."

He says, "You can count on it."

She walks away and the wife asks what that was all about.

The man says, "Well, you might as well know, I'm tired of sneaking around. That was my mistress."

The wife says with a huff, "I want a divorce."

He says, "Ok, but think about that agreement you signed – the house stays, the car stays, the jewelry stays, all the money stays. But I won't be a total ass, I'll set you up in a little apartment until you can find a job to support yourself."

The wife says she'll have to think about that.

Then about that time their friend Harry walks into the restaurant with a beautiful young girl on his arm.

The wife asks, "Who's that with Harry?"

The husband replies, "Well, you might as well know, that's Harry's mistress."

The wife is again flabbergasted but thinks for a minute and says, "You know what? .. Ours is cuter."

The Beginning

First the Lord made man in the Garden of Eden.
Then he said to himself, "There's something he is needin'."
After casting about for a suitable pearl,
He kept messing around and created a girl.
Two beautiful legs, so long and so slender,
Round, slim, and firm, and ever so tender.
Two lovely hips to increase his desire,
And rounded and firm to bring out the fire.
Two lovely breasts, so full and so proud,
Commanding his eyes, as he whispers aloud.
Two lovely arms, just aching to bless you,
And two loving hands, to soothe and caress you.
Soft, cascading hair hung down over her shoulder,
And two dreamy eyes, just to make him grow bolder.
T'was made for a man, just to make his heart sing.
Then he added a mouth, and ruined the whole damn thing!

Quickies

A guy comes home to find his wife missing. He spends the next two days searching frantically for her, only to return home and find her in the kitchen, eating a plate of pasta.

"You're alive!" he exclaims. "Where have you been?"

She replies, "These four men kidnapped me and had wild sex with me for a week."

He says, "But you've only been gone two days."

She says, "Yeah, I'm just here to get something to eat."

A guy says to a blond, "Look at that dog with one eye."

She covers one eye, turns her head around and asks, "Where?"

Infants should enjoy infancy as much as adults enjoy adultery.

The difference between a whore and a slut is a whore will sleep with anyone while a slut will sleep with anyone but you.

Marriage has many pains, but celibacy has no pleasures.

"Honey, I look fat, ugly, and pale. Say something to cheer me up."

He thinks for a second and says, "Well, there's nothing wrong with your eyesight."

I am defending her honor, which is more than she ever did.

Never fry bacon naked.

You only have to mumble a few words in church to be married and a few words in your sleep to be divorced.

Thou shalt not *admit* adultery.

A human being is the best computer available to place in a space craft. It is also the only one that can be mass produced with unskilled labor.

-Werner Von Braun

The most common form of a marriage proposal begins with: "YOU'RE WHAT?"

Sex is a lot like pizza.

When it's good, it's really good and when it's bad it's still pretty good.

The worst BJ that I ever had was wonderful.

Women; they make the highs higher and the lows more frequent.

Beauty is power; a smile, its sword.

If you're afraid of loneliness don't marry.

I never knew what true happiness was until I married, then it was too late.

Marriage means commitment, but then so does insanity.

Men are from Mars Women are from Hell

I want to love you, but how can I, if you won't lay down?

See no evil, hear no evil, date no evil.

What do you call one thousand heavily armed lesbians?

Militia Etheridge

Always get married in the morning. That way, if it doesn't work out it won't ruin your whole day.

If it wasn't for the stock market I wouldn't ever get screwed.

She still misses her ex-husband but her aim is getting better.

What do you do if you find your wife stumbling around in the front yard? Put another bullet in her.

There is proof that blondes are smarter than horses. They don't shit during the parade.

What did one lesbian vampire say to the other? See you next month.

Foreplay is to sex as a long line is to an amusement park ride.

Passing a wedding reception, a guy comments on how beautiful the bride is.

His pal replies, "That's good because she's never going to look any better."

Weddings should be very special occasions. Getting married is something most of us will only do two or three times in our lives.

Thibedeau, he say , "Hey Budreaux. Let's just say . . . that I was to do your wife. And let's just say. . . that she was to have my baby. Would that make you and me . . . like... related?"

Budreaux, he say, "No. . . It'd make us even."

When a man steals your wife there is no better revenge than to let him keep her.

--Sacha Guitry

Observe the mother before you take the daughter.

--Turkish proverb

His wife was very punctual. She bought everything on time.

An old maid knows all the answers, but is never asked the question.

The primary reason women marry is because somebody asked them.

It's a terrible thing to grow old alone. He said his wife hadn't had a birthday for six years.

Suzie was on her way to the airport when she saw a sign that said, Airport Left.

She turned around and came home.

What's the last thing a Polish stripper takes off?

Her bowling shoes.

I didn't have sex with my wife until we were married. How about you?

I don't know – when did you marry her?

What's the difference between dogs and foxes?

About four beers.

Do you talk to your wife after sex?

Yeah, if I have my phone handy.

Men forget but never forgive.

Women forgive but never forget.

A man falls in love thru his eyes; a women thru her ears.

A women's favorite position is CEO.

That's Mrs. Bitch to you!

A hard on doesn't count as personal growth.

"You know, son, if you masturbate too much you'll go blind."

"Over here, Dad."

A lady covered with furs and high dollar jewelry, apparently not accustomed to shopping for groceries rushs with her over loaded cart into the express lane.

A fellow waiting in the regular lane calls to her, "Hey lady, can't you see that that's the express lane?"

"Can't you see that I'm in a hurry?"

Words with Two Meanings

1. THINGY (thing-ee) n. Female.... Any part under a car's hood. Male.... The strap fastener on a woman's bra.

2. VULNERABLE (vul-ne-ra-bel) adj. Female.... Fully opening up one's self emotionally to another. Male.... Playing football without a cup.

3. COMMUNICATION (ko-myoo-ni-kay-shon) n. Female.... The open sharing of thoughts and feelings with one's partner. Male.... Leaving a note before taking off on a fishing trip with the boys.

4. COMMITMENT (ko-mit-ment) n. Female.... A desire to get married and raise a family. Male.... Trying not to hit on other women while out with this one.

5. ENTERTAINMENT (en-ter-tayn-ment) n. Female.... A good movie, concert, play or book. Male.... Anything that can be done while drinking beer.

6. FLATULENCE (flach-u-lens) n. Female.... An embarrassing byproduct of indigestion. Male.... A source of entertainment, self-expression, male bonding.

7 MAKING LOVE (may-king luv) n. Female.... The greatest expression of intimacy a couple can achieve. Male.... Call it whatever you want, just as long as we do it.

8. REMOTE CONTROL (ri-moht kon-trohl) n. Female.... A device for changing from one TV channel to another. Male.... A device for scanning through all 375 channels every 5 minutes.

The Class Reunion

My wife and I were at my class reunion when she noticed a drunken lady sitting alone at a nearby table swigging her drink. She asked if I knew her.

"Yes", I answered, "She's my old girlfriend. I understand that she took to drinking after we broke up those many years ago and hasn't been sober since."

"My God", exclaimed my wife, "Who would think a person could go on celebrating that long?"

Flowers on Friday

Noticing the flowers on her co-worker's desk, she asked, "Who sent you the beautiful roses?"

"My boyfriend", she replied with a groan.

"You don't seem very pleased about the flowers. Why not?"

"When I get roses from him on a Friday, I can expect to spend the weekend on my back with my legs spread>"

"Don't you have a vase?"

He said, She said

He said . . I don't know why you wear a bra; you've got nothing to put in it.

She said . . You wear pants don't you?

He said . . Shall we try swapping positions tonight?

She said . . That's a good idea - you stand by the ironing board while I sit on the sofa and fart!

He said . . What have you been doing with all the grocery money I give you?

She said . . Turn sideways and look in the mirror!

He said . . How many men does it take to change a roll of toilet paper?

She said . . We don't know; it has never happened.

She said . . Why is it difficult to find men who are sensitive, caring and good looking?

He said . . They already have boyfriends.

She said . . What do you call a women who knows where her husband is every night?

He said . . A widow.

Know why there were only forty-nine contestants in the Miss Black America Pageant?

No one would wear the Idaho sash.

And Then it Started

One year, a husband decided to buy his mother-in-law a cemetery plot as a Christmas gift.

The next year, he didn't buy her a gift.

When she asked him why, replied, "Well, you still haven't used the gift I bought you last year!"

And that's how the fight started.

My wife and I were bed watching 'Who Wants to be a Millionaire?' I turned and asked, "Do you want to have sex?"

She said, "No."

"Is that your final answer?

"Yes."

"Then I want to call a friend."

That's when the fight started.

Does this dress make me look fat?

Not as much as the one you wore yesterday.

You guessed it. The fight started.

Male

DRINK

Age 17 Beer
Age 25 Beer
Age 35 Vodka
Age 48 Double Vodka
Age 66 Maalox

HOUSE PET
Age 17 Roaches
Age 25 Stoned-out college roommate
Age 35 Irish Setter
Age 48 Children from first marriage
Age 66 Barbi

SEDUCTION LINE
Age 17 My parents are away for the weekend!
Age 25 My girlfriend is away for the weekend!
Age 35 My fiancee is away for the weekend.
Age 48 My wife is away for the weekend.
Age 66 My second wife is dead.

FAVORITE SPORT
Age 17 Sex
Age 25 Sex
Age 35 Sex
Age 48 Sex
Age 66 Napping

DEFINITION OF A SUCCESSFUL DATE
Age 17 "Tongue"

Age 25 "Breakfast"
Age 35 "She didn't set back my therapy."
Age 48 "I didn't have to meet her kids."
Age 66 "Got home alive."

FAVORITE FANTASY
Age 17 Getting to third base
Age 25 Airplane sex
Age 35 Ménage a trois
Age 48 Taking the company public
Age 66 Swiss maid / Nazi love slave

WHAT'S THE IDEAL AGE TO GET MARRIED?
Age 17 25
Age 25 35
Age 35 48
Age 48 66
Age 66 17

IDEAL DATE
Age 17 Triple Stephen King feature at the drive-in
Age 25 "Split the check before we go back to my place"
Age 35 "Just come over."
Age 48 "Just come over and cook."
Age 66 Sex in the company jet on the way to Vegas.

FEMALE

DRINK
Age 17 Wine Coolers
Age 25 White Wine
Age 35 Red Wine
Age 48 Dom Perignon
Age 66 Shot of Jack with an Ensure chaser

EXCUSES FOR REFUSING DATES
Age 17 Need to wash my hair
Age 25 Need to wash and condition my hair
Age 35 Need to color my hair
Age 48 Need to have Francois color my hair
Age 66 Need to have Francois color my wig

DRUG
Age 17 Shopping
Age 25 Shopping
Age 35 Shopping
Age 48 Shopping
Age 66 Shopping

FAVORITE SPORT
Age 17 Shopping
Age 25 Shopping
Age 35 Shopping
Age 48 Shopping
Age 66 Shopping

FAVORITE FANTASY
Age 17 Tall, dark and handsome
Age 25 Tall, dark and handsome with money
Age 35 Tall, dark and handsome with money and a brain
Age 48 A man with hair
Age 66 A man

DEFINITION OF A SUCCESSFUL DATE
Age 17 "Burger King"
Age 25 "Free meal"
Age 35 "A diamond"
Age 48 "A bigger diamond"
Age 66 "Home Alone"

WHAT'S THE IDEAL AGE TO GET MARRIED?
Age 17 17
Age 25 25
Age 35 35
Age 48 48
Age 66 66

HOUSE PET
Age 17 Muffy the cat
Age 25 Unemployed boyfriend and Muffy the cat
Age 35 Irish setter and Muffy the cat
Age 48 Children from his first marriage and Muffy the cat
Age 66 Retired husband who dabbles in taxidermy and stuffs Muffy the cat

IDEAL DATE
Age 17 He offers to pay
Age 25 He pays
Age 35 He cooks breakfast the next morning
Age 48 He cooks breakfast the next morning for the kids
Age 66 He can chew breakfast

Women's Seminar Topics

The Auto Hood Release, What Is It and Why Is It There
Life Beyond Shoes
Money, The Non-Renewable Resource
How to Get 90 Minutes Out of an Hour
Why Men Don't Like any of Your Friends
How to not be a Victim of Marketing
How to Get Out of Bed Without Waking Up Your Man
Is There Really Enough Makeup in The World
Cigar Smoke and Its Benefits
Clocks and Time: The Mysterious Connection
Tupperware: Its Social and Environmental Drawbacks
Where to Look When Your Auto is in Reverse
Learning When Not to Talk, And Then Not Talking
How to Avoid Turning into Your Mother
Quality Time: When You and Your Husband Should Spend Time Apart
How to Accept Criticism or When to Give up on Cooking
Telltales Sounds Associated With Auto Collisions
Silence, the Final Frontier: Where No Woman Has Gone Before.
The Undiscovered Side of Banking: Making Deposits.
Man Management: Discover How Minor Household Chores Can Wait Until After the Game.
Bathroom Etiquette: His Razor is His.
Driving a Car Safely: A Skill You can Acquire.
Water retention: Fact or Fat.
Cooking I: Bringing Back Bacon, Eggs and Butter.
Cooking II: Bran and Tofu are Not for Human Consumption.
Classic Clothing: Wearing Outfits You Already Have.
Oil and Gas: Your Car Needs Both.
Appreciating the Humor of the Three Stooges.
"Do These Jeans Make Me Look Fat?" - Why Men Lie.

Poetry

I met the perfect woman. Who could ask for anything more?

She's deaf and dumb, loves to fuck, and owns a liquor store.

Toast heard near closing time

Here's to your little thing and my little thing, under the table.

I hope your little thing doesn't need anything 'cause my little thing isn't able.

Here's to the night I met you.

If I hadn't met you, I wouldn't have let you.

Now that I let you, I'm glad that I met you.

And I'll let you again, I bet you!

Here's to men

When I meet them, I like them.

When I like them, I kiss them.

When I kiss them, I love them.

When I love them, I let them.

When I let them I lose them

Here's to all the girls

I love the girl who does, I like the girl who don't.

I hate the girl who says she will, and then decides she won't.

But the girl I like the best of all, and I know you'll say I'm right;

Is the girl who says I shouldn't, but just for you I might.

Here's to the girl I love the best.

I've loved her naked, and I've loved her dressed.

I've loved her standing and I've loved her lying.

And if she had wings, I'd love her flying.

And when she's dead and long forgotten,

I'll dig her up and love her rotten.

Here's to the lovely lady dressed in white

When she smiles, she smiles so sweet

She makes things stand that have no feet.

Here's to the girl with the little red shoes

She spends your money and drinks your booze.

She's lost her cherry, but that's no sin

She's still got the box that the cherry came in.

Holy Mary, we believe that without sin thou did conceive.

Now we pray in thee, believing that we can sin without conceiving.

Here's to nipples. For without them, titties would be pointless.

Four blessings upon you

Older whiskey

Younger women

Faster horses

More money

Marine Corps Drinking Song

Mary Ann Barnes is the queen of all the acrobats, She can do tricks that'd give a man the shits.

She can shoot green peas from her fundamental orifice, do a triple summersault and catch 'em on her tit.

She's a great big son of a bitch, twice as big as you and me,

Hair on her ass like the branches on a tree.

She can run, fight, swim, fuck, roll a barrel and drive a truck.

That's the kind of girl I wanna marry me.

Here's a little Marine Corps trivia

Women Marines are "affectionately" referred to as "BAMs"- Broad Ass Marines. Male clerks are known as "ball bearing BAMs".

More Quickies

New invention: A vibrating tampon. A woman can be at her best when she's at her worst.

Did you know Helen Keller had a pony?
She didn't either.

My old business partner said he had a sweater picked out for me as a Christmas present. I told him I'd rather have a screamer, or at least a moaner.

What do all the battered wives have in common?
They just don't listen.

What do you call a woman with two black eyes?
Nothing, she's already been told twice.

Why a woman doesn't need a watch?
There's a clock on the stove.

Why are women's feet smaller than men's?
So she can stand closer to the sink.

Why do brides wear white?
Most kitchen appliances are white.

Why did God create women?
He couldn't teach the sheep to bring him a beer.

In my opinion, giving birth is nothing compared to being circumcised. I was circumcised at a very young age. I don't remember much about it but I do know that afterwards I couldn't walk for about a year.

Getting hit in the testicles is more painful than childbirth. I can prove it. Did you ever hear of a man volunteering to get hit in the testicles?

A naked woman jumps into a cab and tells the cabbie to take her to the nearest hotel.

The cabbie asks, "Since you're naked, how are you going to pay the fare?"

She spreads her legs and asks, "Will this cover it?"

He asks, "You got anything smaller?"

If men gave birth, we'd all be only children.

What does a blonde ask after having multiple orgasms?

You guys all on the same team?

A man and woman were discussing whether men or women enjoy sex the most.

"Obviously men enjoy sex more. Look at how hard we work to get laid," the man argues.

"No", the woman retorts. "Think about when your ear itches. You put your finger in your ear and wiggle it around. Which feels better, your finger or your ear?"

A nurse stops by a bank to cash a check, totally exhausted after an eighteen hour shift. When she goes to take out her pen to endorse the check, she finds she has a rectal thermometer in her hand.

"That's just great," she groans, "Some asshole's got my pen."

At a Weight Watcher's meeting, a lady complains to the lady next to her, "My husband insists I come to these meeting because he likes to screw somebody with a trim figure."

Her friend asks, "What's wrong with that?"

"He screws her while I'm at these meetings

A perfect woman

She's three feet tall. Her ears are pistol grips and when you twist them, her mouth opens and her teeth fold back. She's got a flat head where you can set a six pack. When you're done she has a pizza delivered, tidies up the place and leaves.

"The fellow was explaining to his soon to be married friend how he should never take any guff from his new bride. "My wife stared yelling at me for spending too much money at happy hour. Then she started cussing me. I said to her, "How'd you like not to see me for three days?"

She said, "Oh, sure."

"Well, the next day she didn't see me. The second day she didn't see me. On the third day, she could see out of one eye, just a little bit."

I remember seeing Roseanne on TV years ago when she went by the name of Roseanne Barr. and she would say in her best nasal voice,

"My husband is sitting on the couch in front of the TV and he calls out, 'Roseanne, we got any Doritos chips?'

"Like he can't lift up the cushions and look for himself."

Dear Mom

This is the joke that my mother laughed the hardest at during her last years. I had to be careful telling her jokes. They needed to be just a tiny, tiny bit dirty, and this one was just perfect.

A fellow goes to a reunion and he looks across the crowded room and sees this beautiful woman. He's pretty sure that she was the girl that he was tremendously infatuated with in school but never had the nerve to approach.

So he musters his courage, goes up to her and says, "You know, you look like Helen Brown."

She looks him over and says, "You don't look so hot in blue either."

My mother did tell me this one. As a young boy I thought it was wonderfully risqué.

Little Audrey comes home and she has a handful of nickels. Her mother asks her where she got those nickels. And she says the little boys gave them to her to see her hang by her knees from the tree limb.

Her mother says, "Little Audrey, don't you know those boys are just giving you nickels to see your panties?"

Little Audrey just laughed and laughed, because she knew she wasn't wearing any panties.

Graffiti

For refund, insert baby here - *on a condom machine*

If Barbi is so popular why do you have to buy all her friends?

Sex is the most beautiful natural thing money can buy.

No body's perfect. . . well, there was this one guy, but we killed him.

Woman's rule of thumb; If it has tires or testicles, you're going to have trouble with it. -Women's restroom wall, Dick's Last Resort, Dallas, Texas

Willie Nelson's favorite joke – he says it really happened

Roger Miller walks into a Cadillac dealership in Nashville. The salesman recognizes him and greets him, "Good afternoon, Mr. Miller. Are you thinking about getting a new Cadillac?"

Roger answers, "No! I'm going to get a new Cadillac! I'm thinking about pussy."

Speaking of Willie, I found a profound comment made by America's favorite country singer/songwriter:

"Ninety nine percent of the world's lovers are with their second choice. That's what makes the jukebox play."

Freudian Slip

Two fellows are talking and one guy says, "Gosh, I had a Freudian slip this morning."

Guy number two says, "You know, I've heard that term many times but I've always been too embarrassed to ask. What is a Freudian slip?"

First guy: "It's a psychological term but it's really pretty simple. It's when you say what you're thinking instead of what you meant to say. For instance this morning there was a very buxom young lady at the ticket counter wearing a tight sweater with the top buttons open.

I said to her, "Give me two pickets to Tittsburgh."

The second guy says, "Oh yeah, I see what you mean. I had a Freudian slip this morning at breakfast. I meant to say to my wife, "Please pass the plate of buttered toast."

But instead, I said, "You fucking bitch, you ruined my life."

Apparently PMS has been around forever. It's even referenced in our most famous bible story:

"And Mary rode Joseph's ass all the way to Bethlehem."

Profound Thoughts

Ben Affleck says to his psychiatrist, "Every time I look in the mirror, I get an erection."

The psychiatrist replies, "I'm not surprised. You're a pussy."

Nine out of ten men prefer women with big breasts; the tenth guy prefers the other nine.

Getting married is like going to lunch with friends. You're happy about what you ordered until you see what the others got.

God says to Adam I have some good news and some bad news.

The good news is I've given you a brain and a penis.

The bad news is you only have enough blood to operate one at a time.

God has some more good and bad news for Adam.

Adam, the good news is I'm giving you sex.

The bad news is I've put women in charge of it.

Men who treat women as helpless and charming playthings deserve their women who look at them as delightful and generous bank accounts

Late one night he's pulled over by a cop who asks if he's been drinking.

"Why do you ask? Is there a fat girl in the car?"

Why don't elephants use tampons?

You wouldn't either if you had to put them in and take them out with your nose.

How do you tell when an elephant's having its period?

Your mattress is missing.

Asking a tall guy if he plays basketball is like asking a fat lady if she sings opera.

The local slut went to London only to discover that Big Ben is just a clock.

Mother asked little Susie what happened at playschool today. She says, "Tommy showed me his pee pee."

Mother was about to faint when Susie continued that it reminded her of a peanut.

Mother sighs a little sigh of relief and says, "Small, huh?"

Susie says, "No, salty."

Now, Mother faints.

I actually heard this comment from a blonde, "The battery in my cell phone lasts pretty long unless I'm making long distance calls."

An older lady was very despondent and asked the doctor where the best place would be to shoot herself, if she wanted to commit suicide. The doctor replied below your left breast. She shot herself in the thigh.

Viagra will soon be available in liquid form, and will be marketed by Pepsi Cola as a power beverage suitable for use as a mixer.

It will now be possible for man to literally pour himself a stiff one. Obviously we can no longer call this a soft drink, and it gives new meaning to the names of 'cocktails', 'highballs' and just a good old-fashioned 'stiff drink'. Pepsi markets the new concoction by the name of: "Mount-n-Do"

.Bubba met his wife at a tobacco spiting contest.

He figured if she'd put that nasty stuff in her mouth he could put most anything in there he wanted to.

Oysters are not a very good aphrodisiac. I ate a dozen one night and only six worked.

Women like a man who is tall, dark and has some.

More on the toilet seat; after all it was part of the keynote of this book.

Girls, accept responsibility. The very first time you fall into the water you might get away with blaming the guy. But seriously, any time after that, getting upset with anyone other than your self is childish and irresponsible. As I said earlier, it shows stupidity.

If you fall into the water on a regular basis, have some self respect and don't tell anybody.

Finally, it's been brought to my attention by Shubnell that women never think of how considerate the guy is to lift the lid, in the first place, to make sure not to pee on the seat.

Deserted Island

On a trans-pacific flight the plane goes down leaving only two survivors; Ernie and the current playmate of the year. Basically unharmed, they wash up on a beautiful deserted island. There is shelter there with an abundance of fruit, fish and game. It's paradise.

It turns out the playmate and Ernie get along great and become lovers, existing alone in a Garden of Eden. Life is good.

One day Ernie says, "While I'm really happy to be here with you I hope you can understand that I miss having another guy to talk to once in a while."

She agrees to put on his shirt so they can go for a walk and he can pretend to talk to his old buddy, Pinkerton.

Ernie gets into the scene, puts his arm around "Pinkerton" and says, "Gosh, it's good to see you old friend. There's so much I want to tell you. First of all, you won't believe who I'm fucking."

Speaking of deserted islands, two guys and a beautiful girl are marooned on this tiny island. Things were going okay until the girl died. Finally the guys started feeling guilty about what they were doing and they buried her.

Then they started feeling so guilty about what they were doing that they dug her up.

Women's Vocabulary Lesson for Men

Fine: This is the word women use to end an argument when they are right and you need to shut up.

Five minutes: If she is getting dressed it means half an hour. Five minutes is only five minutes when you have been given five more minutes to watch the game before helping around the house.

Nothing: This is the calm before the storm. This means "Something" and you should be on your toes. Arguments that begin with "Nothing" usually end with "Fine".

Go ahead: This is a dare, not permission. Don't do it.

Loud sigh: This is not actually a word, it is a nonverbal statement often misunderstood by men. A "loud sign" means she thinks you are an idiot and is wondering why she is wasting her time standing there arguing with you over nothing.

That's Okay: This is one of the most dangerous statements a woman can make to a man. "That's okay" means she wants to think long and hard about how she's going to make you pay for your mistake.

Thanks: A woman is thanking you, period. Do not question it or faint. Just say "You're welcome."

Whatever: A woman's way of saying #@&* you!

Riddles

See if you can figure out the second answer to these riddles

What's the difference between a girl's track team and a tribe of pygmies?

One is a bunch of cunning runts.

What's the difference between an epileptic cornhusker and a prostitute with diarrhea?

One shucks between fits.

What's the difference between a woman in church and a prostitute in a bathtub?

One has hope in her soul.

Some Differences

I was married for seven years.

It seemed like seven minutes; underwater

A man runs over a woman – whose fault is it?

It's the man's – he shouldn't have been driving in the kitchen.

Make love not war. Hell do both, get married.

The young hillbilly tells his pa that he's not going to marry the young girl from over the mountain. When his pa asks why not, he says he found out that she's a virgin.

"That's the thing to do, boy. If she ain't good enough for her own family she sure ain't good enough for ours."

The boy did take a bride and the old man hikes up to their honeymoon cabin to visit. He walks in to find the boy vigorously masturbating.

"What the hell are you doing, boy? You got a pretty young wife to take care of that kind of thing."

"I know daddy, but her poor little arm just gets so tired."

What do you call room full of women, half with PMS, half with yeast infections?

A whine and cheese party.

UCLA STUDY

A study conducted by UCLA's Department Psychiatry has revealed that the kind of face a woman finds attractive on a man can differ depending on where she is in her menstrual cycle.

For example: If she is ovulating, she is attracted to men with rugged and masculine features.

However, if she is menstruating, or menopausal, she tends to be more attracted to a man with duct tape over his mouth and a spear lodged in his chest while he is on fire.

No further studies are expected at this time due to a shortage of male volunteers.

A sweet little girl is eating a snack cake as she waits in the barbershop for her daddy.

The barber says, "Darling, you're going to get hair on your Twinkie."

"I know", she smiles, "I'm going to get boobies, too."

An invisible man marries an invisible woman. Their children weren't much to look at.

Two antennas met on a roof and got married. The ceremony wasn't much but the reception was excellent.

The author, Joseph Wambaugh, referred to a female detective as "Dickless Tracy".

Eating Out:

If Claire, Louise and Hannah go out to lunch, they will call each other Claire, Louise and Hannah. If Russell, John and Trevor go out they will affectionately refer to each other as Jackson, Parrot Face and T.C. (*Top Cat from the 1970's cartoon series*)

When the bill arrives, Russell John and Trevor will each throw in $20 when the bill is only $32.50. None will have anything smaller and none will actually admit that they want change back.

When the girls get their bill, out come the pocket calculators.

A man has seven items in his bathroom: toothpaste, toothbrush, a can of shaving cream, a razor, a bar of soap, some deodorant, and a pilfered hotel towel.

The average number of items in a typical woman's bathroom is 337. A man should not be able to identify more than 20 of these items.

Arguments:

A woman has the last word in any argument. Anything a man says after that is the beginning of a new argument.

Success:

A successful man is one who makes more money than his wife can spend. A successful woman is one who finds such a man.

Women love cats. Men say they love cats, but when the woman isn't looking they'll kick the cat.

A woman worries about the future until she gets a husband.

A man never worries about the future until he gets a wife.

Eternity; the time that passes between when you come and she leaves.

By the time a man has money to burn, the fire has gone out.

Young girls will tell you, look but don't touch. As they get older you hear the opposite.

Beauty is only a light switch away.

Marriage is a hopeless endeavor. If you think about the conflicting expectations, it's a wonder any marriages last:

A woman marries a man expecting he will change. A man marries a woman expecting she won't change. They're both disappointed.

A fellow is pretty sure he has his young Labrador retriever trained when he stops by the market to pick up some items. It's a beautiful day, not too hot. He thinks he can trust his pup to stay in the car with the windows rolled down. As he walks toward the entrance to the store, he repeatedly turns and states in a stern voice toward the car, "Stay. Stay."

A young blonde coming from the other direction notices this and asks, "Why don't you just put it in park?"

There's an upside to dating a homeless girl. After the date you can drop her off anywhere.

The story is that a on a dare, a young short timer Marine pinched Eleanor Roosevelt's ass. This led her to describe Marines as, "A bunch of underpaid, over sexed teenage killers."

Damn, that made us proud.

I know of mothers who put their teenage daughters on birth control pills. Think about the message this sends. Every morning when that girl takes her pill, she is reinforcing that, yes, she can have sex today.

Then again, she might turn out to be a sweet little girl who only has sex twice in high school – the football team and the band.

The Texas woman was asked in court why she shot the thief six times in the back as he fled with her purse.

She answered, "Because when I pulled the trigger the seventh time all it did was go click."

She was acquitted.

Did you hear about the morning after pill for men?

It changes his blood type.

This next one came from a source who wishes to remain anonymous. I just want you all to know that it's not from me.

Why is it a good thing that men fall asleep after sex?

So women can properly finish the job

There was this deformed girl in high school. She had one tit, right in the middle of her back.

We all felt sorry for her, but she sure was fun to slow dance with.

Speaking of deformed girls, did you hear about the girl with one boob larger than the other?

She won first and third place in the wet t-shirt contest.

Dickins' Fruit Stand

Jimmy Bob Dickins runs a family owned fruit stand just outside Dallas. It's famous for its homemade apple cider. Women seem to particularly enjoy this cider.

I know one gal who says she can't go for more than a week without some Dickins' cider.

Say the last line again, out loud if you need to.

Money Making Idea

Find a bar that will let you put a condom machine in the ladies' room. The beauty of this scheme is you don't have keep condoms in it. The ladies will be too embarrassed to ask for their quarters back.

Gotta Love Southwest Airlines

We're at the finals for the Miss International Flight Attendant contest. They bring out the first finalist while the other two are in a sound-proof booth so they can ask each one the same question.

The question is actually a situation where the plane has crashed in deepest, darkest Africa and she awakens to find herself surrounded by 40-50 fierce native warriors, each sporting a huge erection.

The contestant is then asked, "Given the situation, how would you handle this problem?"

The first finalist, Miss American Airlines, says she would commit suicide before she would allow herself to be ravaged by these savages.

The next finalist, Miss United Airlines, says she would pick out the biggest, toughest one of the bunch and give herself to him hoping he would protect her from the rest of them.

Finally, it's Miss Southwest Airlines' turn. She answers, "I understand the situation, but what's the problem?"

Christmas Ham

A young newlywed was preparing a ham for Christmas dinner. She carefully cut off the end of the ham prior to pacing it in the pan for baking.

Her husband asked her, "Why did you cut off the end of the ham?"

She replied, "I really don't know. My mother always did it so I thought you were supposed to."

Later when talking to her mother she asked why she cut off the end of the ham before baking it.

Her Mother replied, "I don't know. That's how my Mother always did it."

A few weeks later while visiting her Grandmother, the young woman asked, "Grandma, why is it that you cut off the end of the ham before baking it?"

Her Grandmother replied, "Well, dear, otherwise, it would never fit into my baking pan."

Cheating Wife

There is a joke that surprised me. Because it is a little off color and involves a cheating wife I really expected at least some ladies to be offended by it. Quite the contrary, almost all the ladies I've told this to found it hilarious.

A fellow flags a cab at the airport. As he gets in the cab, he says to the cabbie that he's coming home a day early because he really thinks he can catch his wife cheating on him. If the cabbie will come in with him and act as a witness, there's an extra $100 in it for him. The cabbie agrees.

They get to the fellow's house, hurry to the bedroom and throw the covers off the bed. Sure enough, there's the wife in bed with some strange man. The husband pulls out a pistol, holds it to the man's head and says, "I'm going to blow you away."

The wife jumps up and says, "No, don't do that. He's really a good guy. I didn't inherit any money like I told you. He gave me the money to pay off the house. He gave me the money to buy you that new Corvette. He gave me the money for the membership at the fancy country club so you can play golf. He even pays the monthly dues."

The husband turns to the cabbie and says, "Damn, I don't know what to do now."

The cabbie answers, "Well . . . if I were you. . . I'd cover his ass up before he catches a cold."

The Young Air Policeman

To his credit, a former neighbor told me this story on himself.

After growing up in a small town, this shy and very inexperienced young man joined the Air Force. He got accepted into and completed Air Police school.

On his first day patrolling by himself, he catches a lady speeding down a stretch of road that is just outside the fence but still on Air Force property.

At this point our naïve young man is quite confident in his starched uniform, spit shined jump boots, arm band, baton, pistol, helmet, sunglasses, etc. He's looking like a modern SS storm trooper.

The lady, although a little older, is quite attractive so he decides he should say something cool. He approaches the car and asks, "Where's the fire?"

She looks up at him, straight in the eye, and responds, "It's right here between my legs and I don't think you've got enough hose to put it out."

Absolutely flustered, all he can manage to stammer is 'Okay'.

He turns, head down, quickly walks back to his jeep and drives away.

It was seven years before he told anyone this story.

Golf Story

Dewight comes into the clubhouse where his friend Roger asks him how his round of golf went. Dewight responds with a barely audible, raspy voice, "It was the worst round of golf I ever had."

Roger says, "My God, man, you can hardly talk. What happened to your voice?"

Dewight says, "Well, we were behind this foursome of ladies. Each one of them sliced their ball into that cow pasture.

I asked if we could play through and they said sure. I got up there and damned if I didn't slice my ball into the cow pasture too.

So I'm out there looking for my golf ball and these four ladies are looking for their golf balls. I see this old broke down milk cow and every time the cow's tail swished I see this little flash of white. I went up behind the old cow and sure enough, wedged up in there was a Titleist. I wasn't playing a Titleist today.

I asked the lady closest to me as I lifted up the cow's tail, 'Does this look like yours'?

"She hit me right in the throat with her club."

Divorce

A man takes his wife out for their silver anniversary dinner and asks, "What would you like for our anniversary? You can have anything you want – a new car, a mink coat, a diamond necklace, just name it."

The wife replies, "I want a divorce."

The husband is stunned and finally replies, "Damn! I wasn't planning on spending that much."

Why are divorces so expensive?

Because they're worth it.

"I put my SOB ex-husband through medical school," says Woman 1.

Woman 2 says, "That's nothing, I made my ex-husband a millionaire."

Woman 1 asks, "What was he before?"

Woman 2 replies, "A billionaire."

Poor Farmer

A farmer is selling peaches door to door when a particularly well built lady answers her door wearing a nearly sheer nightgown.

She cups one full breast and asks, "Are those peaches as tender and ripe as this?" A tear wells up in one eye as he answers, "Yes".

She lets her gown fall open, lightly runs her fingers over her crotch and purrs, "Is the fuzz on those peaches as soft and silky as this?" Now tears run down both cheeks as he answers, "Yes".

The lady asks him, "Why are you crying?"

The farmer sobs, "A drought took my wheat crop, a flood took my corn crop and now you're going to fuck me out of my peaches."

The Road Trip

While on a road trip, an elderly couple stops at a restaurant for lunch. The finish their meal and resume their trip.

When leaving, the woman unknowingly left her glasses on the table.

She didn't miss them until they had been driving about 40 miles. To add to the aggravation, they had to travel quite a distance before they could find a turnaround in order to return to the restaurant to retrieve her glasses.

All the way back, the elderly husband became the classic grouchy old man. He fussed and complained and scolded his wife during the entire drive. The more he chided her, the more agitated he became. He wouldn't let up for one minute.

To her relief, they finally arrived back at the restaurant.

As the woman got out of the car and hurried to retrieve her glasses, the old geezer yelled at her, "While you're in there you might as well get my hat and the credit card. "

Texas Gal

On a lighter note, a Texas girl settles into her seat for a long plane ride. She introduces herself to her seatmate and asks, "So, where're y'all from?"

The woman replies, quite icily, "I am from a place where people are intelligent enough to not use a preposition to end a sentence."

"I see", replies our Texas gal, "So…where're y'all from... bitch?"

The same Texas gal ends up seated by another Yankee. This one is an arrogant professor who figures this pretty young thing with the drawl can't be too smart so he'll have some fun and impress her with his superior intelligence.

He suggests, "To pass the time perhaps we could have a conversation. Would you like to discuss something, say, nuclear physics?"

She says, "Sure, but first let me ask you a question. The droppings from a rabbit are little pellets, the horse produces cylindrical wafer-like manure while cattle manure splatters into a pie like mess.

Why are there these differences? They all eat grass?"

The professor says that he has no idea.

Our Texas gal replies, "How do y'all expect to discuss nuclear physics when y'all admit that y'all don't know shit?"

While at the mall, our Texas gal is delighted when her boyfriend stops in front of a jewelry store and begins looking at engagement rings. He asks how large the stone should be.

She replies, "Honey, this is Texas. A diamond is like hair. You caint git it too big."

A broad from New Jersey answered the same question with,

"Haff a carat, haff a man."

Mommy, where did you meet Daddy?

We met at a party.

Was I with you then?

No but you were with me when I went home.

Haven't I seen you somewhere before?

Yeah, you're the reason I don't go there anymore.

Love is not a feeling.

It's a skill

Costume Party

In preparation for the big costume party the wife goes to a shop and gets costumes for her and her husband.

Just as they are about to dress for the party, the wife starts feeling sick. She tells her husband that she's not well enough to go and that he should go on without her.

"Oh no, baby, you know I can't have any fun without you", he says.

This goes back and forth for a while until she finally convinces him to go on alone.

He takes his costume, to change into at the party.

Soon after he leaves the wife starts feeling better and comes up with an idea. She'll put on her costume and go to the party. Since she knows what he's wearing and he doesn't know what she'll be wearing, this could be fun. He won't know she's there and she can see if he really can't have any fun without her.

She arrives at the party and soon spots her husband, dancing with every pretty girl there. She is well disguised and soon she's dancing with her husband who's unaware of who she is.

They dance up a storm and next thing you know they've off to a dark corner and having a quick but hot bout of sex.

She slips away, unrecognized, hurries home, puts her costume away and gets in bed pretending to read a book as she waits for her husband.

When he gets home she's anxious to hear what he has to say about the party. "Did you have good time", she asks.

"Baby, you know I can't have any fun without you."

"That's sweet. Did you at least get to dance?"

"No, to tell the truth, I never danced one dance. As soon as I got there I got into a poker game inside and played until the party was over.

But the guy I lent my costume to said that he had a hell of a time."

Be Careful Cheating on a Southern Woman

A Southern woman came home unexpectedly and caught her husband in bed with another woman. With super-human strength, borne of fury and chopping firewood, she dragged him by his genitals, through the house, out the back door, across the yard and into the tool shed.

She then put his willie into a vise, tightened it securely and removed the vise's handle.

When she picked up an old rusty carpenter's saw, the husband screamed, "Please don't saw it off!"

"Oh, I'm not going to saw it off." She put the saw in his hand and as she picked up a can of kerosene and a box of matches, she continued, "I'm going to set the shed on fire. You can do whatever you want".

Frank Feldman

As the cab comes around the corner a guy steps out of an office building and flags the cab just as it approaches him.

He gets into the taxi and the cabbie says, "Perfect timing. You're just like Frank."

Passenger: "Who?"

Cabbie: "Frank Feldman. He's a guy who does everything right all the time. Like my coming around the corner just as you need a cab. Things like that always happen to Frank."

Passenger: "There are a few dark clouds over everyone."

Cabbie: "Not Frank. He was a terrific athlete. He could have won the Grand Slam in tennis. He could golf with the pros. He sang like an opera baritone, danced like a Broadway star and you should have heard him play the piano. He was an amazing guy."

Passenger: "Sounds like he was really special."

Cabbie: "That's not all. He had a memory like a computer. He remembered everyone's birthday. He knew all about wine, which foods to order and which fork to use. He could fix anything. Not like me. I change a fuse and the block goes dark. Frank could do everything right. No one could ever measure up to Frank."

Passenger: "What a fellow. How did you meet him?"

Cabbie: "Oh, I never met him. He died. I married his widow."

It was a slow rainy day at the car dealership and the salesmen were sitting around trying to out do one another with stories of their successes with the ladies.

Joe, the clean up guy, wanting to join in, says, "I figure that I've totally satisfied every woman that I've ever been with."

The salesmen ask him to explain.

"It's simple. Not a one of them ever asked for more."

The husband was watching TV from the couch and hears his wife ask, "What would you like for dinner, love, chicken, lamb or beef?"

"I think I'd like to have lamb, thank you."

"You're having left over spaghetti, I was asking the cat."

George W.

Remember when President George W. Bush made an official visit to Great Britain? The red carpet was rolled out with all the pomp and circumstance that only the British can muster.

Four beautifully groomed purebred horses pulled George W. and Queen Elizabeth in the golden royal carriage. Midway to Buckingham Palace, the horse closest to the Queen passed gas that wilted every flower within a twenty yard radius.

"Mr. President, I am so embarrassed", said the Queen.

"Your Majesty, you are such a lady", said George W. "If you hadn't said nothing, I'd a sworn the horse did it."

She was only a whisky maker, but I love her still.

There's an upside to dating a homeless girl.

After the date you can drop her off anywhere.

Women with Big Breasts

- Can get a taxi on the worst days and have a neat place to carry spare change

- Always has been the center of the arts.

- Make jogging a spectator sport

- Can keep a magazine dry while laying in the tub

- Usually can find leftover popcorn after a movie

- Always float better

- Know where to look first for lost earrings

- Rarely lack for a slow dance partner

- Have a place to set their glasses when sitting in an armless recliner

Women with Small Breasts

- Don't cause a traffic accident every time they bend over in public

- Find that dribbled food makes it to the napkin on their lap

- Can always see their toes and shoes

- Can sleep on their stomachs

- Have no trouble sliding behind the wheel of small cars

- Know that people can read the entire message on their t-shirts

- Can come late to a theater and not disturb the entire aisle

- Can take aerobic class without running the risk of knocking themselves out.

- And. . . . you can get closer to them.

Short Ones

An old friend, is a top financial appraiser and business consultant. He says women are depreciating assets; however they can be very costly to get rid of.

He also offers a business rule: "If it flies, floats, or fucks; lease it – don't buy it."

Why is a girl from Oklahoma like a tornado? Either one will take your mobile home.

At dinner with a blonde, the guy mentions that she has something on her cheek.

She wipes at her right cheek.

"Other side", he says.

She wipes the inside of her right cheek.

Every time I walk into a singles bar I can hear Mother's wise words:

"Don't pick that up. You don't know where it's been."

To be happy with a man you must love him a little and understand him a lot.

To be happy with a woman you must love her a lot and try not to understand her at all.

Four guys are playing golf and the ladies in front of them are playing extremely slow. They're getting very frustrated and finally one fellow volunteers to go up and ask if they can play through. He gets about halfway there and then turns around and comes back.

The other golfer asks, "What's the matter?" The first guys answers, "My god, one of those ladies is my wife and the other one is my mistress."

So the other fellow says he will take care of it. He heads toward the ladies, gets about halfway there and then he turns around and comes back.

The first guy asks, "What's the matter?" and the other fellow says, "Small world."

I married my wife for her looks, but not for the ones she's been giving me lately.

I saw a woman with a sweatshirt with the word "GUESS" on it.

I guessed, "Implants?"

Marriage changes passion. . . Suddenly you're in bed with a relative.

The Polish girl tells her mother that she's pregnant.

"Oh my God," shrieks the mother, "But, wait. Are you sure it's yours?"

A man needs a mistress just to break the monogamy.

A man isn't so afraid of committing to one woman as he is afraid of forgoing all the other women.

When I get home from work just a little late, my wife is all over me, raising hell. You often stay out till all hours and never seem to have any trouble. How do you do it?

When I get home after chasing around, I screech into the drive, slam the garage door open and close, slam doors, turn on lights, stomp into the bedroom, throw my shoes into the corner, then slap the wife on the ass and loudly say, "Roll over baby. Your tiger's home".

She never wakes up.

Maria Gets a Raise

Maria, a maid, goes to the lady of the house and asks for a raise.

Lady: Why do you think you deserve a raise?

Maria: There are three reasons. First of all I iron better than you.

Lady: Says who?

Maria: Your husband. He also said that I'm a better cook.

Lady: Oh? What's your third reason?

Maria: I'm a better lover than you.

Lady: Don't you dare tell me that my husband told you that too.

Maria: No. The pool boy told me that.

Lady: How much do you want?

Getting a Ticket

A man and his wife were driving on the highway when a state trooper pulls them over. He asks for his license and registration.

"I'm sorry officer. What seems to be the problem?"

Officer: "I clocked you on radar going 75 miles an hour."

Man: "There must be some mistake, I was only going 65."

Wife: "Oh Harold, you were going at least 80."

Officer: "I'm also citing you for having a tail light out."

Man: "It must have just gone out. I checked them this morning."

Wife: "Oh Harold, I told you two months ago it was out."

Officer: "I'm also citing you for not wearing a seatbelt."

Man: "But Officer, I just took it off as you were approaching my car."

Wife: "Oh Harold, you know you never wear your seatbelt."

Man: "Listen you stupid #@*%. Shut your #@!*(%* mouth."

Officer: "Ma'am, does he always talk to you this way?"

Wife: "Only when he's drunk."

How to keep a blonde busy forever.

"Go to the next page"

How to keep a blonde busy forever, continued.

"See previous page"

Sorority Girls

How many sorority girls does it take to change a light bulb?
One, she holds on to it and the world revolves around her.

What three words will a sorority girl never hear?

Attention K-Mart shoppers.

What is a sorority girl's favorite position?

Facing Neiman Marcus.

How do you get 4 sorority girls on one chair?

Tell them there is a rich guy sitting on it.

Why does a sorority girl close her eyes during sex?

So she can fantasize about shopping.

What is the difference between a sorority girl and Jell-O?

Jell-O wiggles when you eat it.

What do you call a sorority girl's water bed?

Lake Placid.

How do you know when a sorority girl is a nymphomaniac?

She will make love the same day she got her hair done.

What do you say to a sorority girl that won't give it up?

Have another beer.

What is a sorority girl's mating call?

I'm soooooo drunk.

How can you tell if a sorority girl has had an orgasm?

She drops her nail file.

How do you stop a sorority girl from having sex?

Marry her.

Did you hear about the new sorority girl doll?

You put a ring on her finger and her hips get bigger.

How do you get a former sorority girl in your bed?

Grease her hips so she'll fit through the door and throw a Twinkie on the bed.

Two nuns are riding their rickety old bikes down the back streets of Rome late one afternoon. As it starts to get dark, one is becoming a little nervous. She leans over to the other and says, "I've never come this way before."

The other one replies, "I think it's the cobblestones."

"Miss, what do you suggest as a gift for my younger, single, rich and handsome brother?", he asked the pretty clerk.

"My phone number", she purred.

Women will fake an orgasm for the sake of a relationship. Men will fake a relationship for the sake of an orgasm.

She said she wasn't a proctologist, but she knew an asshole when she saw one.

Public Works

Two blonde girls were working for the city public works department. One would dig a hole and the other would follow behind her and fill the hole in.

They worked up one side of the street, then down the other, then moved on to the next street, working furiously all day without rest, one girl digging a hole, the other girl filling it in again.

An onlooker was amazed at their hard work, but couldn't understand what they were doing. So he asked the hole digger, "I'm impressed by the effort you two are putting in to your work, but I don't get it -- why do you dig a hole, only to have your partner follow behind and fill it up again?"

The hole digger wiped her brow and sighed, "Well, I suppose it probably looks odd because we're normally a three-person team, but today the girl who plants the trees called in sick."

Women's Rules

The female always makes the rules.

The rules are subject to change at any time without prior notification.

No male can possibly know all the rules.

If the female suspects that a male knows any of the rules, she must immediately change some or all of the rules.

* **The female is never wrong.**

If the female is wrong, it is because of a flagrant misunderstanding which was a direct result of something the male said or did wrong.

If the previous rule applies the male must apologize immediately for causing the misunderstanding.

* **The female can change her mind at any given point in time for any reason.**

The male must never change his mind without express written consent from the female.

* **The female has the right to be angry or upset at any time.**

The male must remain calm at all times unless the female wants him to be angry or upset.

The female must not under any circumstances let the male know whether or not she wants him to be angry or upset.

Any attempt by the male to document these rules could result in severe bodily harm.

*   **If the female has PMS all rules are null and void.**

The barn burned down on the older couple's farm. Since it was insured for fifty thousand dollars the wife called their insurance agent to ask him to send them a check for that amount.

"Oh, that's not how it works," he says. We'll replace your old barn."

"Oh my, if that's how it works, you'd better cancel my husband's life insurance."

A guy went up to two young ladies in a singles bar and offered each of them a thousand dollars to spend the night with him.

One stormed off in a huff. The other stayed calm, cool, and collected.

Men's Rules

1. Breasts are for looking at and that is why we do it. Don't try to change that.

2. Learn to work the toilet seat. Be a big girl. If it's up, put it down. We need it up. You need it down. You don't hear us complaining about having to put it up.

3. Saturday = Sports. It's like the full moon or the changing of the tides.

4. Shopping is not a sport and we will never think of it that way.

5. Crying is blackmail.

6. Ask for what you want. Let us be clear on this one: subtle hints do not work, strong hints do not work, and obvious hints do not work. JUST SAY IT.

7. "Yes" and "No" are perfectly good answers to almost every question.

8. Come to us with a problem only if you want help solving it. That's what we do. Sympathy is what your girlfriends are for.

9. A headache that lasts seventeen months is a problem. See a doctor.

10. Anything thing we said six months ago is inadmissible in an argument. In fact, all comments become null and void after six days.

11. If you think you're fat, you probably are. Don't ask.

12. If something we said can be interrupted two ways and one way hurts your feelings, we meant the other one.

13. You can either ask us to do something or you can tell us how it's done, not both. If you already know how to do it, do it yourself.

14. Whenever possible, please say whatever you have to say, during commercials.

15. Christopher Columbus didn't need directions and neither do we.

16. ALL men see in only sixteen colors, like windows default settings. Peach, for example is a fruit, not a color. Pumpkin is a vegetable. We have no idea what mauve is.

17. If it itches, it will be scratched. We do that.

18. If we ask what's wrong with you and you answer "nothing", we will act like nothing's wrong. We know you are lying but it's just not worth the hassle.

19. If you ask a question you don't want an answer to, expect an answer you don't want to hear

20. When we have to go somewhere, whatever you wear is fine. Really!

21. Don't ask us what we're thinking about unless you are prepared to discuss such topic such as; sex, sports, or cars.

22. You have enough clothes.

23. You have too many shoes.

24. I am in shape. Round is a shape.

Thank you for reading this. I know I have to sleep on the couch tonight, but did you know men really don't mind that? It's like camping.

Thoughts from Groucho

*   Women should be obscene and not heard.

*   I never forget a face but in your case I'll be glad to make an exception.

*   I've had a perfectly wonderful evening. But this wasn't it.

*   The husband who wants a happy marriage should learn to keep his mouth shut and his checkbook open.

*   How do you feel about women's rights? I like either side of them.

*   Politics doesn't make strange bedfellows. Marriage does.

*   Marriage is the chief cause of divorce.

*   Paying alimony is like feeding hay to a dead horse.

*   Any one who says he can see through a woman is missing a lot.

*   I love everything about you; your lips, your eyes, your hair. The only thing I can't stand is you.

*   Some folks claim that marriage interferes with romance. There's no doubt about it. Anytime you have a romance, your wife is sure to interfere.

A Woman's Perfect Breakfast

She's sitting at the table enjoying her gourmet coffee.

Her son is on the front of the Wheaties' box.

Her daughter is on the cover of Business Weekly.

Her boyfriend is on the cover of Playgirl and her husband is on the back of the milk carton.

How do you explain that a woman can take boiling hot wax, pour it on their upper thighs, tear out the hair by the roots, and still be afraid of a spider?

What do you call a lesbian with ten girlfriends?

A bush hog.

How many men does it take to open a beer?

None.. It should be open when she brings it to him.

Good Time Sally had to be buried in a 'Y' shaped coffin.

The Beltline Office

TNT Sports Page located on Belt Line Road in North Dallas is affectionately known as the Belt Line Office by those fortunate enough to be able slip away for some afternoon cocktails.

Sandy Miller, the manager and day bartender, and I have developed a little comedy routine over the years.

Me: Hey Sandy, you're a student of sociology and psychology – tell me which do you think is our most important problem, ignorance or indifference?

Sandy: I don't know and I don't care.

Me: Hey Sandy, do you like to cuddle after sex?

Sandy: No. I like to get my money and go home.

Me: Hey Sandy, do you smoke after sex?

Sandy: Only if I do it too fast.

Me: Hey Sandy, what would you do if I told you tomorrow was Easter?

Sandy: I'd start coloring eggs.

Me: Hey Sandy, where's grandma?

Sandy: She's back at the ranch beating off the Indians.

Me: No wonder they keep coming back.

Me: Hey Sandy, what do you think about that guy?

Sandy: The gate's down, the lights are flashing, but there's no train coming.

Me: Not too bright, huh?

Sandy: Yeah, the wheel's spinning, but the hamster's dead.

Me: Hey, Sandy, were you a good girl in school?

Sandy: Of course I was. I only had sex twice – the football team and the band.

Me: Hey, Sandy, does your sister still work at the orange juice factory?

Sandy: No. She got canned.

Me: Oh?

Sandy: Yeah. She couldn't concentrate

Me: Hey Sandy. what's the first thing you know?

Sandy: First thing you know, old Jed's a millionaire. . .

Me: Hey Sandy, what happened twenty years ago?

Sandy: It was twenty years ago today, Sergeant Pepper taught the band to play. . .

Me: Hey Sandy, are you busy?

Sandy: I'm so busy, I can't procrastinate until tomorrow.

Me: Hey Sandy, you ever have trouble making a decision?

Sandy: Well, yes and no. Could I get back to you tomorrow on that?

Me: Hey, Sandy, I heard you were going to open a whorehouse upstairs.

Sandy: Nah. Too much fucking overhead.

Many of the regulars have urged us to take this act on the road. I was saddened to learn it wasn't meant as a compliment.

Still Got a Sense of Humor

One day an aging waitress announced to everyone and no one in particular that she was a very lucky girl.

She said, "Yep, I'm a lucky girl. I'm living my dream. Not many people get to live their dream. When I was a little girl I used to dream that someday I would grow up, get married, have a family, get divorced, and spend the rest of my life working as a cocktail waitress."

Making love - It's what women are doing when the guy is getting laid.

Baby, I wouldn't lie to you unless I really cared about you.

There are only two four letter words offensive to men - don't" and "stop", unless they're used together.

Impotence - Nature's way of saying, "No hard feelings."

A guy is pulled over by a cop who says, "Did you know your wife fell out about two miles back?"

The man replies, "Thank God. I thought I was going deaf."

Bill Clinton had some pretty bad luck. He hooked up with a Jewish girl who couldn't get out a stain.

Don't you think that Dick Cheney should have been impeached when he shot that judge in the face while bird hunting?

After all Clinton got impeached when he shot somebody in the face.

Here's another thought: If Clinton had known how good Hillary would be at blowing the presidency, he wouldn't have needed Monica.

Why did the woman cross the road?

Better question: Why is she out of the kitchen?

What do you call a woman with two brain cells? Pregnant

What is six inches long, has a head on it and drives women crazy?

Money.

How can you tell if a woman has an orgasm?

Who cares.

Why hasn't a woman gone to the moon?

It doesn't need cleaning yet.

The wife found her husband sitting on the back porch crying. "What's wrong," she asked.

He answers, "Do you remember when we were dating and your father told me that if I didn't marry you he would send me to prison for 20 years?"

"Yeah, so what", she replied.

"I would have gotten out today," he sobbed.

Why do women fake orgasms?

They think we care.

Why do women like intelligent men.

Opposites attract.

What do you call an intelligent woman in America?

A tourist.

Some mornings I wake up grouchy. Some mornings I just let her sleep.

A man is incomplete until he is married.

After that he is finished.

How is marriage like a hot bath?

After you get used to it, it's not so hot.

Wife: The two things I cook best are meatloaf and apple pie.

Husband: Which one is this?

What's worse than a male chauvinist pig?

A woman who won't do what she's told.

What is the difference between a battery and a woman?

A battery has a positive side.

Virginity can be cured.

What is love?

The delusion that one woman differs from another.

Why did God make lesbians?

So feminists couldn't breed.

To you lesbians and virgins: Thanks for nothing.

How many men does it take to fix a vacuum cleaner?

Why the hell should we fix it? We don't use the damn thing.

Wife - An attachment you screw on the bed to get the housework done.

How are women like parking spaces?

The good ones are taken and the rest are handicapped.

Women say that men are like parking spaces too.

The good ones are taken and the rest are too small.

Did you hear they finally made a device that makes cars run 95% quieter?

Yeah, it fits right over her mouth.

Why do women have boobs?

So men will talk to them.

What's the difference between a pre-menstrual feminist and a terrorist?

You can reason with a terrorist.

How many feminists does it take to change a light bulb?

Two; one to complain about the man who made it and one to call the electrician.

Man of the House

The husband had just finished reading a new book entitled, 'You can be the man of your house'.

He stormed to his wife in the kitchen and announced, "From now on, you need to know that I am the man of this house and my word is law. You will prepare me a gourmet meal tonight, and when I'm finished eating my meal, you will serve me a sumptuous dessert.

After dinner, you are going to go upstairs with me and we will have the kind of sex that I want. Afterwards, you are going to draw me a bath so I can relax. You will wash my back and towel me dry and bring me my robe. Then, you will massage my feet and hands.

Then tomorrow, guess who's going to dress me and comb my hair?

The wife replied, "The funeral director would be my first guess."

Great Women's Tee-Shirts

Remember my name; you'll be screaming it later.

Don't worry; it'll only seem kinky the first time.

Of course I don't look busy, I did it right the first time.

I'm multi-talented. I can talk and piss you off at the same time.

Don't start with me. You will NOT win.

You have the right to remain silent so please shut up

All stressed out and no one to choke

If we are what we eat, I'm fast, cheap and easy

And your point is. . .

Next mood swing; 5 minutes

I hate everybody. You're next.

I'm busy. You're ugly. Get lost.

If you're going to ride my ass, at least pull my hair

Warning: I have an attitude and I know how to use it.

Zero to bitch in 3 seconds

Obey me! You'll be happier.

I'm bad and you love it!

Yet, despite the look on my face, you're still talking.

I refuse to have to have a battle of wits with an unarmed person.

SL_T; all I need is U

Give peas a chance

It's all about me

If you can't afford to tip, you can't afford to drink.

I don't sweat. I glisten.

I tried being good. It didn't work out.

Your trailer park called. Their trash is missing.

Don't hate me because I'm beautiful. Hate me because I have big tits.

Did you eat a bowl of stupid for breakfast?

I'm sorry honey; I can't hear you without a drink in my hand

You look like I need another drink

Guns don't kill people. Dads with pretty daughters do.

Huh? I didn't hear you. I was too busy being awesome.

I'm what Willis was talkin' 'bout.

Sarcasm is one more service I offer

I'm trying to imagine you with a personality

Don't worry I forgot your name too

One of us is thinking about sex... okay it's me

It ain't the size, it's... No it's the size

Do it right the first time and maybe I'll let you do it again

Don't shake me, don't wake me, just take me!

I'll try to be nicer if you'll try to be smarter.

I'm a virgin. (*This is a very old shirt*)

I'm not your type. I'm not inflatable.

I am a virgin. I'm just not very good at it.

Be naughty. Save Santa the trip.

Dream when you're asleep, role play when you're awake.

Even if you understood, you'd never believe it.

Erotic, exotic and a wee bit psychotic...

If you can't enjoy yourself, enjoy somebody else.

Oral sex is the answer. The question doesn't matter

You may not remember me, I'm dressed now.

Don't you think it's about time you tried me?

If you're not into oral sex keep your mouth shut

Readthiswhileyoustareatmytits

Evita Peron, first lady of Argentina, at a formal dinner in London, commented, "My husband and I work tirelessly for our people, yet many call him a thief and they even call me a whore."

A gentleman at her table responded, "Madame, pay it absolutely no mind. Personally, I left the sea years ago but many persist in calling me Admiral."

Bette Midler in her best Shophie Tucker voice: "My boyfriend Ernie and I were in bed last night and he said, Shoph, you got no tits but a tight box."

"I said to him, I said, Ernie, get off my back."

My boyfriend, Ernie, says to me, "Let me tell you something, Shoph. On my eightieth birthday, I'm going to marry me a twenty year old girl. What do you think of that?"

I said, "Ernie, I think that's wonderful, but Ernie let me tell you something. On my eightieth birthday, I'm going to marry me a twenty year boy. And let me tell you something else Ernie, twenty goes into eighty a hell of a lot more than eighty goes into twenty."

The more pregnant I get, the more strangers smile at me. Why's that?

You're fatter than they are.

Good girls get to go to heaven.

Bad girls get to go everywhere.

Try this one if you want to see a redhead smile,

"A girl without freckles is like a night without stars."

I was commenting to a girl at the Beltline Office that while there are some jokes that women do find funny, there is a large number of jokes that women don't think are funny at all.

Her dry response was, "Yeah, you've told me those."

I'm not saying that she's slow but it takes her two hours to watch Sixty Minutes.

She went on a diet for two weeks. Lost fourteen days.

One Liners

I learned to lick from a lesbian. - Man's tee-shirt

My goal in life is to satisfy the world's nymphomaniacs.

I fully support women's lib, sweetmeat.

It takes two heterosexuals to make one homosexual.

One who objects to being a sex object probably couldn't be.

Sex is only the business of the pile of people involved.

A cheap dominatrix would offer bargain debasement.

Cunning linguists do it with words.

Few men look trustworthy with their pants down.

Flip over, I want a puppy.

Love is blind, especially love at first sight.

The only proven aphrodisiac is money.

I'm thinking that she is a virgin. . .or at least she used to be.

Losers always whine about how they did their best.
 Winners go home and fuck the prom queen.

Some guys are born on third base and act like they hit a triple.
- Barry Switzer

It only takes one beer to get me drunk, usually it's the eleventh one.

Vampires give killer hickies.

For a taste of religion-lick a witch

If you can read this the bitch fell off. - *on the back of a biker's tee shirt*

More people are violently opposed to fur than leather because it's safer to harass rich women than motorcycle gangs.

Virginity; use it you lose it.

On average everybody has one testicle.

I love sex. It's free and doesn't require special shoes.

69 is head over heels in love

Women fake orgasms, men fake foreplay.

It's not premarital sex if you don't get married.

The blonde calls across the river to her friend, "How do I get to the other side?"

Her blonde friend answers, "Duh! You are on the other side."

A blonde accepts the handsome stranger's invitation to come home with him. She follows in her car through a dark and winding route to his house.

After a night of love making he awakens her to explain that he must leave for an early meeting. "Sleep as long as you like," he tells her. "There's plenty to fix for breakfast. Just lock up when you leave."

Cooking breakfast, she somehow manages to start a fire in the kitchen and calls 911 for the fire department.

"What's your address?" they ask.

She replies, "I don't know."

"Can you tell us how to get there?"

"Duh! Get in your big red truck and drive!"

Almost had a psychic girlfriend, but she left me before we met.

Bigamy is when two rites make a wrong.

Kinky sex involves the use of duck feathers.

Perverted sex involves the whole duck.

Two wrongs don't make a right but three rights can make a left.

So, he said to his irate girlfriend, "Who lit the fuse on your tampon?"

What are the three biggest tragedies in a man's life? Life sucks, job sucks, and the wife doesn't.

Despite the old saying, 'Don't take your troubles to bed', many men still sleep with their wives.

Life's a bitch. A good life is a lot of bitches.

Abortion, love's labor lost.

Whatever you give a woman, she will make greater. She multiplies and enlarges what is given to her.

If you give her sperm, she'll give you a baby.

If you give her a house, she'll give you a home.

If you give her groceries, she'll give you a meal

If you give her a smile, she'll give you her heart.

So, if you give her any crap, be ready to receive a ton of shit."

Virginity is not dignity, its lack of opportunity.

A mistress comes between mister and mattress.

An English teacher wrote on the blackboard; Woman without her man is nothing and asked the students to punctuate so it made sense.

The boys wrote: Woman, without her man, is nothing.

The girls wrote: Woman! Without her, man is nothing.

For Christmas, he got her a lot more than she got him.

She got him a sweater. He got her pregnant.

Pissed her off so bad she started her period.

A man is sunbathing naked at the beach. For the sake of civility and to keep his privates from getting sunburned he covers them with his hat.

A woman walks by and says with a snicker, "If you were a gentleman you'd tip your hat."

He replies, "If you were better looking, it'd tip itself."

Men wake up in the morning as good looking as ever.

Women somehow deteriorate during the night.

Dancing is wonderful training for girls: It's the way to guess what a man is going to do before he does it.

Ginger Rogers did everything Fred Astaire did, except she did it dancing backwards in high heels.

The seven dwarves of menopause:

Itchy, Bitchy, Sweaty, Sleepy, Bloated, Forgetful and Psycho

Hanoi Jane

"If you understood what communism was, you would hope, you would pray on your knees we would one day become communist."

-Jane Fonda speaking to University of Michigan Students, 1970

"I'm a very brave person. I can go to North Vietnam, I can challenge my government, but I can't challenge the man I'm with if it means I'm going to end up alone."

"If you're ever in a situation where you're not getting served or not getting what you need, just cry."

"Working in Hollywood does give one certain expertise in the field of prostitution."

"It hurt so many soldiers, it galvanized such hostility, it was the most horrible thing I could have possibly done. It was just thoughtless."

-Jane Fonda expressing regret for posing on the North Vietnamese anti-aircraft guns.

If I had my way, Miss Fonda would be coming up for parole about now.

Note: Fonda has been married three times. All her husbands cheated on her.

Don't be sexist! Bitches hate that.

If your dog is barking at the back door and your wife is yelling at the front door, which do you let in first?

The dog. He will shut up once you let him in.

What do you call a woman who has lost 95% of her intelligence?

Divorced.

Scientists have discovered a food that diminishes a woman's sex drive by 95%. It's called wedding cake.

Marriage is a three ring circus.

Engagement ring, wedding ring, suffering.

Our last fight was my fault. My wife asked what's on TV and I said "dust."

A beggar walked up to a well dressed woman shopping on Rodeo Drive and said, "I haven't eaten anything in 4 days."

The woman looked at him and replied, "God, I wish I had your willpower."

The most effective way to remember your wife's birthday is to forget it once.

Women will never be equal to men until they can walk down the street with a bald head and beer gut and still think they're beautiful.

There are two theories to arguing with women.

Neither of them work.

Says he suspects that his wife is dead?

Says the sex is the same but the dishes are piling up.

How many divorced women does it take to screw in a light bulb?

One to screw in the bulb and three to form a support group.

Think about this: No matter how beautiful she may be, sometime, somewhere, some guy got tired of her.

Here's a thought: Einstein, arguably the smartest man ever, got divorced.

Later he married his cousin with the big tits.

Perfect example of the two different heads doing the thinking.

I've concluded that women have three types of orgasms:

There's the affirmative orgasm. "Yes, Yes!"

Then there's the spiritual orgasm. "Oh God, Oh God!"

Finally there's the fake orgasm. "Oh Chapman, Oh Chapman!"

On reading this, Tom Shubnell claimed to have witnessed woman's perfect orgasms when she screams. "Oh Tom, Oh Tom!"

Yeah, sure!

Everyone cannot have the best health care.

Laws of statistics tell us that half the doctors will always be below average.

Women are Vindictive

As the lady was fumbling through her purse at the store the clerk noticed a TV remote. "Do you always carry a TV remote?" asked the clerk.

"No," she replied. "My husband refused to go shopping with me so I figured this was the most evil, legal thing I could do to him."

I told my wife that a man is like a fine wine; he gets better with age.

She locked me in the cellar.

Women are like guns.

Keep one around long enough and you're going to want to shoot it.

Buying your wife a gun is saying, "I want to kill myself but I kind of want it to be a surprise".

Manly Test

1. In the company of females, intercourse should be referred to as:

 a) lovemaking

b) screwing

c) the pigskin bus pulling into tuna town

2. You should make love to a woman for the first time only after you've both shared:

 a) your views about what you expect from a sexual relationship

 b) your blood-test results

c) five tequila slammers

3. You time your orgasm so that:

a) your partner climaxes first

 b) you both climax simultaneously

 c) you don't miss Sportsworld

 4. Passionate, spontaneous sex on the kitchen floor is:

a) healthy, creative love-play

b) not the sort of thing your wife/girlfriend would ever agree to

c) not the sort of thing your wife/girlfriend need ever find out about

5. Spending the whole night cuddling a woman you've just had sex with is:

a) the best part of the experience

b) the second best part of the experience

c) $100 extra

6. Your girlfriend says she's gained five pounds in weight in the last month. You tell her that it is:

a) no concern of yours

b) not a problem, she can join your gym

c) a conservative estimate

7. You think today's sensitive, caring man is:

a) a myth

b) an oxymoron

c) a moron

8. Foreplay is to sex as:

a) appetizer is to entrée

b) primer is to paint

c) a line is to an amusement park ride

9. Which of the following are you most likely to find yourself saying at the end of a relationship?

a) "I hope we can still be friends."

b) "I'm not in right now, please leave a message at the beep."

c) "Welcome to Dumpsville, population, YOU."

10. A woman who is uncomfortable watching you masturbate:

a)   probably needs a little more time before she can cope with that sort of intimacy

b) is uptight and a waste of time

c) shouldn't have sat next to you on the bus in the first place

RESULTS

If you answered "a" more than 7 times, check your pants to make sure you really are a man.

If you answered "b" more than seven times, check into therapy, you're still a little confused.

If you answered "c" more than 7 times, "YOU DA MAN!"

How to Get Along

Everybody knows that there are days when all a man has to do is open his mouth and he takes his life in his hands! This is a handy guide that should be as common as a driver's license in the wallet of every husband, boyfriend, or significant other!

Dangerous	**Safer**	**Safest**	**Ultra Safe**
What's for dinner?	Can I help you with dinner?	Where would you like to go for dinner?	Here, have some wine.
Are you wearing that?	Wow, you sure look good in brown.	Wow, look at you.	Here, have some wine.
What are you so worked up about?	Could we be overreacting?	Here's my paycheck.	Here, have some wine.
Should you be eating that?	You know, there are a lot of apples left.	Can I get you a piece of chocolate with that?	Here, have some wine.
What did you do all day?	I hope you didn't overdo it today?	I've always loved you in that robe.	Here, have some wine.

Advice from Men to Women

Never buy a 'new' brand of beer because it was on sale.

If we're in the backyard and the TV in the den is on, that doesn't mean we're not watching it.

Don't tell anyone we can't afford a new car. Tell them we don't want one.

Whenever possible please try to say whatever you have to say during commercials.

Please don't drive when you're not driving.

Don't feel compelled to tell us how all the people in your stories are related to one another. We're just nodding, waiting for the punch line.

The quarterback, who just got pummeled, isn't trying to be brave. He's just not crying. Big difference!

When the waiter asks if everything is okay, a simple 'Yes' is fine.

Why do ladies' magazines like Cosmopolitan, waste time with surveys on what women want in a man? They always conclude that women want caring, thoughtful, kind, and sensitive men.

Then they fall for the bad boy.

A diplomat is a man who can convince his wife she looks vulgar in diamonds and fat in a mink coat.

Diplomacy is remembering her birthday and forgetting her age.

All that's needed for a divorce is a wedding.

He who marries for money, earns it.

He who gets a dowry with his wife, sells himself for it.

The girl who is easy to get may be hard to take.

Feminism: A socialist, anti-family political movement that encourages women to leave their husbands, kill their children, practice witchcraft, destroy capitalism, and become lesbians.

Alimony - The screwing you get for the screwing you got.

True Story Received from an English Professor

You know that book Men are from Mars, Women from Venus? Well, here's a prime example of that. This assignment was actually turned in by two of my English students: Lisa and Dave from English 44A, California State University, Hayward, Creative Writing, Prof. Miller. The In-class Assignment for Wednesday:

Today we will experiment with a new form called the tandem story. Each person will pair off with the person sitting to his or her immediate right. One of you will then write the first paragraph of a short story. The partner will read the first paragraph and then add another paragraph to the story. The first person will then add a third paragraph, and so on back and forth. Remember to re-read what has been written each time in order to keep the story coherent. The story is over when both agree a conclusion has been reached.

And now, the assignment as submitted by Lisa & Dave:

Lisa starts:>   At first, Laurie couldn't decide which kind of tea she wanted. The chamomile, which used to be her favorite for lazy evenings at home, now reminded her too much of Carl, who once said, in happier times, that he liked chamomile. But she felt she must now, at all costs, keep her mind off Carl. His possessiveness was suffocating, and if she thought about him too much her asthma started acting up again. So chamomile was out of the question.

Dave: Meanwhile, Advance Sergeant **Carl Harris**, leader of the attack squadron now in orbit over Skylon 4, had more important things to think about than the neuroses of an air-headed asthmatic bimbo named Laurie with whom he had spent one sweaty night over a year ago. "A.S. Harris to

Geostation 17," he said into his transgalactic communicator. "**Polar orbit** established. No sign of resistance so far..." But before he could sign off a bluish particle beam flashed out of nowhere and blasted a hole through his ship's cargo bay. The jolt from the direct hit sent him flying out of his seat and across the cockpit.

Lisa   He bumped his head and died almost immediately, but not before he felt one last pang of regret for psychically brutalizing the one woman who had ever had feelings for him. Soon afterwards, Earth stopped its pointless hostilities towards the peaceful farmers of Skylon 4."Congress Passes Law Permanently Abolishing War and Space Travel." Laurie read in her newspaper one morning. The news simultaneously excited her and bored her. She stared out the window, dreaming of her youth - when the days had passed unhurriedly and carefree, with no newspapers to read, no television to distract her from her sense of innocent wonder at all the beautiful things around her. "Why must one lose one's innocence to become a woman?" she pondered, wistfully.

Dave   Little did she know, but she has less than 10 seconds to live. Thousands of miles above the city, the Anu'udrian mother ship launched the first of its lithium fusion missiles. The dim-witted wimpy peaceniks who pushed the Unilateral Aerospace Disarmament Treaty through Congress Had left Earth a defenseless target for the hostile alien empires who were determined to destroy the human race. Within two hours after the passage of the treaty the Anu'udrian ships were on course for Earth, carrying enough firepower to pulverize the entire planet. With no one to stop them, they swiftly initiated their diabolical plan. The lithium fusion missile entered the atmosphere unimpeded. The President, in his top-secret mobile submarine headquarters on the ocean floor off the coast of Guam, felt the inconceivably massive explosion which vaporized Laurie and 85 million other Americans. The President slammed his fist on the conference table. "We can't allow this! I'm going to veto that treaty! Let's blow' em out of the sky!"

Lisa: This is absurd. I refuse to continue this mockery of literature. My writing partner is a violent, chauvinistic, semi-literate adolescent.

Dave: Yeah? Well, you're a self-centered tedious neurotic whose attempts at writing are the literary equivalent of Valium.

Lisa: Jerk.

Dave: Idiot.

Perfect Day for a Man

6:00 Alarm.
6:15 Blowjob.
6:30 Massive dump while reading the sports section.
7:00 Breakfast.
Filet Mignon, eggs, toast and coffee.
7:30 Limo arrives.
7:45 Bloody Mary en route to airport.
8:15 Private jet to Augusta, Georgia.
9:30 Limo to Augusta National Golf Club.
9:45 Play front nine at Augusta, finish 2 under par.
11:45 Lunch.
2 dozen oysters on the half shell.
3 Heinekens.
12:15 Blowjob.
12:30 Play back nine at Augusta, finish 4 under par.
2:15 Limo back to airport.
Drink 2 Bombay martinis.
2:30 Private jet to Nassau, Bahamas.
Nap.
3:15 Late afternoon fishing excursion with topless female crew.
4:30 Catch world record light tackle marlin -1249 lbs.
5:00 Jet back home.
En route, get massage from naked supermodel.
7:00 Dinner.
Lobster appetizers, 1963 Dom Perignon, 20 Oz.
New York strip steak.
9:00 Relax after dinner with 1789 Augler Cognac and Cohiba Cuban cigar.
10:00 Have sex with twin 18 year old nymphomaniacs.
11:00 Massage and Jacuzzi.
11:45 Go to bed.

11:50 Let loose a 12 second, 4 octave fart.
Watch the dog leave the room.
11:55 Laugh yourself to sleep.

Perfect Day for a Woman

8:15 Wake up to hugs and kisses.
8:30 Weigh 5 lb.
lighter than yesterday.
8:45 Breakfast in bed, fresh squeezed orange juice and croissants.
9:15 Soothing hot bath with fragrant lilac bath oil.
10:00 Light workout at club with handsome, funny personal trainer.
10:30 Facial, manicure, shampoo, and comb out.
12:00 Lunch with best friend at an outdoor cafe.
12:45 Notice ex-boyfriend` wife, she has gained 30 lbs.
1:00 Shopping with friends.
3:00 Nap.
4:00 A dozen roses delivered by florist.
Card is from a secret admirer.
4:15 Light workout at club followed by a gentle massage.
5:30 Pick outfit for dinner.
Primp before mirror.
7:30 Candlelight dinner for two, followed by dancing.
10:00 Hot shower. Alone.
10:30 Make love.
11:00 Pillow talk, light touching and cuddling.
11:15 Fall asleep in His big, strong arms.

Made in the USA
Charleston, SC
12 February 2010